ALIBI MIKE
AND HIS GANG OF
PARASITES
ON THE STATE

The Experiences of a Fisheries Biologist's
First Summner in Alaska

KIM FRANCISCO

PRISTINE
PRESS AND MEDIA

ISBN
978-1-964804-67-5 (Paperback)
978-1-964804-66-8 (eBook)
978-1-964804-68-2 (Hardback)

Alibi Mike
and his gang of
Parasites
on the State

Kim Francisco

TABLE OF CONTENTS

INTRODUCTION

Wildlife management majors at the university of Alaska, are or were required to work at least 6 weeks in a job related to the major to it a degree. I had transferred to Alaska's University my junior year after completing my sophomore year at grand view junior college in my home town Des Moines, Iowa. During my junior year at U of A, like everyone in Wildlife, I spent my time completing a rewsume, visiting the local Alaska Department of Fish and Game (ADF&G), US Fish and Wildlife Service (USFWS), Bureau of Land Management (BLM) and Alaska Workforce Development Office, to name a few, collecting applications, and job notices. After completing the applications, we would call and try to set-up an interview. A biologist doing a moose research project for the Game Division of ADF&G in Fairbanks thought I was a good fit for the Game tech job he was hiring for the summer. We did all the paperwork and sent it to HQ in Juneau.

Back on campus, amongst the Wildlife students, I was envied for having lined up such and exciting job. I was crushed during finals week, Dr. Cody called and said HQ had rejected my hire since I would only have been in Alaska for ten months not the required twelve.

I spent the summer working day jobs off the day labor bench at Alaska's Workforce Development office in Fairbanks. One day my father called. One of his clients in Iowa was Green Construction. He had gotten me an interview with their Fairbanks office.

I was uncomfortable about "pulling strings" and started my interview poorly apologizing for using influence and not being an Engineering major. My interviewer stopped me, "Who you know may get you a job but what you know will let you keep it. College teaches some people how to think, your major doesn't really matter. Now let's start over."

I ended up an assistant job office manager. Nothing to do with Engineering. I did well enough that after we finished the paving job near Denali National Park. Instead of laying me off they kept me on an airport paving job in Fairbanks. They let me work flex hours so I could return to classes. I was a busy boy.

❦

January of my senior year found me once again delivering resumes and applications by hand and by mail. I was hearing a lot polite were sorry we just don't have any openings or silence.

The Commercial Fisheries Division of the Alaska Department of Fish& Game hires a large number of temporary fisheries technicians every summer. To that end they held an annual job fair on campus. I had skipped the event the year before because I thought I had a job collaring moose. Warm& fuzzy always topped cold& slimy for most prospective biologists. This year I was in line with all the other aspiring Fisheries and Wildlife Biologists waiting for my turn to step in for an interview.

Each person leaving the interview room, we questioned: "Did you get a job?" The smiling ones, rare, answered "Yea I'm hired. Going to Bristol Bay" or some other remote place. But most shrugged "I don't know, they said "maybe but we have a lot of interviews to do" which probably means no."

The few women among us came out looking pretty discouraged or angry. Usually saying something like "Same damn excuses, we don't have separate facilities, girls aren't strong enough, girls distract the boys. "You tell em, that's the damn boy's problem. I'm not a girl but a woman. Outhouses are unisex. I'm stronger than most boys." (This from a first-string basketball player, who probably was stronger than most of us). They take the app, but you can tell they won't hire you."

My father had told me always treat women the way you'd want your mother or sister to be treated. These guys hadn't heard that growing up I guess.[1]

As I neared the front of the line we could see most of the interviewers and began discussing who we hoped we got. There were six interviewers. One interviewer was not much older than us with long shaggy hair seemed

---

[1] Rae Baxter, the one with the long beard, was the exception. He hired women which resulted in a lot of untruthful gossip. The real reason was he and his wife had graduated together with fisheries degrees but she had a terrible time getting a job in the field. At that time Rae was on a campaign to change hiring in the field.

to always have a pleasant smile. We all agreed he was the one we wanted. Three were middle aged, clean shaven with neatly trimmed hair, your basic man on the street. Next was a scary fellow, tall, his face completely hidden by a full beard that when he stood to stretch covered his belt buckle. Last was a tall man, rigidly erect, clean shaven, dressed in slacks instead of jeans with an open collared dress shirt. Looked like he started to wear suitcoat and tie then choose not to or had removed them. Perhaps to fit in when he saw how his companions were dressed. His face never changed expression, just the same cold constant stare. Instead of making one pile of the applications from applicants, his were in two neat piles, one large, rejects we were sure, and one very small pile, the lucky ones? We all agreed he was not the interviewer to get.

"Next" the shaggy one called as Scott walked past us thumbs up saying "I aced it." Jim the last person in front of me answered the call, obvious relief on his face. I was next in line. Yep, the statue called next, I straightened my back and walked over being careful not to shuffle.

"Good Morning Sir, I'm Kim Francisco, here's my application and resume. My first name is Richard but I use my middle name Kim" *Someday you'll start using me instead of that crybaby Kim and avoid these stupid explanations. Richard get over it I need you now to keep me firm and on point.[2]*

"Mike Geiger. Give me both." he answered in a low voice. I sat down in the chair provided and he started running over my paper work, circling things in red every now and then. He quickly scanned the resume but stopped on my description of my job the previous summer as an assistant job office manager for a construction company, underlining and circling some items in it. *All the attention he was giving resume is a good thing, I think.* Then he looked up and said "Sounds like you had to do a lot of calculations in that job last summer?"

"Yes, I mastered the basic stuff in the first couple of days. So, Mr. Howk[3] tried me on the time sheets, which had to be right, because the workers let you know if they aren't. Then there was checking the invoices, I was amazed at the number of suppliers who tried to pad the invoices." *Stop rattling on, scared not sure what to say, **enough, shut up!***

---

[2] Meet two of my three constant mental companions.

[3] Pronounced Hawk.

"OK" Mr. Geiger interrupted. *Richard was right as usual.*

"You may be hearing from me. Send the next one in."

I got up, saying "good bye" since I had been dismissed. A little dejected I headed for the door. Max, who had walked up to the Ridge with me, was next and whispered as we passed "He put yours in the small pile."

❧

I was surprised one morning when Max's voice woke me, calling me to the phone. Stumbling down the cold hallway floor in just my boxer shorts I took the phone from Max. *My family was never going to get the time zone difference between Des Moines and Fairbanks right.*

"Francisco, Mike Geiger, Yukon Area biologist. You interviewed with me last week." Body memory kicked in and I stood to attention, no longer leaning against the wall. "I have a job as a fish ticket editor (*What the hell was that, hope it's in that list of job descriptions they gave us.*), it's in Emmonak at the mouth of the Yukon. It's a Tech III and lasts 3 months. It's hard detailed paperwork and sampling salmon for AWL information (*what?*) do you want the job?"

"YES" I answered as excited as if I had won the lottery, which I sort of had.

"Good, I'll send you a hiring packet to fill out in the mail. Goodbye."

"Wait I have a few questions."

"Do you want the job?"

"Yes but"

"Fine, I'll send the hiring packet for you to read and fill out. It should answer your questions. If you still have some you can call me or wait until orientation. Goodbye." "Bye." *Not a big talker I guess. This is great, like he said the hiring packet should answer most questions. Not like they haven't done all this before so its old stuff to them. Wonder how you spell Emmonak? Never heard of it, need to see if I can find it on a map. Where do I have a map? Who cares I have a job!*

Finals over, Max, Phil (Max's roommate), and I packed our gear into my Land Cruiser and drove to Phil's family home in Anchorage. We spent a couple of days at Phil's. His father kindly showed me a spot next to the driveway where I could leave El Coyote, my LC, for the summer. Max and I finished buying recommended gear on the equipment list that came with

4

our hiring packets. Phil, an electronic engineer major, was working in an electronic repair shop in Anchorage for the summer.

While shopping in Anchorage I discovered the Book Cache, a book store like I had never seen before. I bought everything my remaining checking account balance allowed. A translation of the Koran, most of Norman's Gor novels and some others I've forgotten.

Orientation was two days of training in the Anchorage office. Mostly how to do paperwork and a half day deputation class. The deputy class was interesting because of the antidotes used to illustrate points but consisted mainly of how to record a crime you witnessed and call a real Fish& Wildlife Protection officer. We were not to confront or arrest offenders.

They showed us A-W-L; age-weight-length sampling was all about, its misnamed almost no one records weight anymore. You can get a much better average weight from the fish tickets, a receipt the Department supplies to the fish buyers. A-W-L sampling was really collecting the right scale, there is a patch of scales located by dropping a line from the rear of the dorsal fin and raising another line from the front of the anal fin, then take the scale from the four rows above the median line between these two lines. These are the first scales to grow so by reading the growth rings you can age the fish. The next day, I said goodbye to Max, who was working for a different region. Mr. Geiger put myself and a stranger on a Wein Air flight to Bethel.

The airlines used Boeing 737 jets for the flights to Bush Alaska. They have a moveable wall that separates the passengers from the freight. The freight flies in first class. Passengers have a single class behind the freight; the wall is slid back towards the tail to leave just enough room for seats needed for the passengers on that flight. You clearly know your status, last class, after the freight.

There were only three rows of seats on our flight, the rest of the plane was freight. The stranger, Mike Blanchard, was to be the other fish ticket editor with me in Emmonak. He wasn't excited about the job. He wanted to fish during his off hours. Geiger had made it clear that there weren't any angling opportunities in Emmonak. Mike had already requested a transfer. Geiger was looking for someone who wanted to switch.

The following stories are some of my memories of that first summer that introduced me to my life long career, a new culture, and Alaska. A place so big, wonderful and different that a lifetime isn't enough to experience it all.

FIRST GEAR CHARLIE

My reading was interrupted by the office door bursting open and a frantic man rushing in "Arrest. Come throw out! It's my fish camp! You arrest!"

"Hi I'm Kim Francisco. Have a seat. Would you like a cup of coffee or tea? Then we can talk about your problem." I said hoping to calm the man so I could get his story.

"I'm Charlie. My fish camp. Mine for twenty years. Everyone knows mine. You help. Make leave." He continued as I poured him a cup of joe.

I set the big white porcelain cup down and pulled out a chair. "Have a seat and start your complaint at the beginning." Charlie sat and began spooning sugar into his coffee. Geiger's instructions on handling members of the public seemed to be working. Charlie was smaller than most of the Yup'ik men I had seen in the village. About five two, black hair, brown eyes, maybe

140 pounds soaking wet. Even excited his English was better than most of the Yup'ik commercial fishermen I had talked too.[4] *Hey they know two languages, you don't.*

Charlie took a sip of very sweet coffee and a deep breath. "I load boat last night. Morning go fish camp. Big people from Unalakleet were camped there. Already had buoy anchored in net site.[5] They had tent on my frame. Some fish cut and drying on my racks. They told me to get out or they would beat me. I left." Charlie had started calmly but was now getting worked up again. "That fish camp mine. You make leave!"

Luckily, the crew-leader of our Flat Island test fishery, had explained some of the differences between the Yukon set net fishery and the set net

---

[4] It would be another ten or twelve years before Alaska Department of Fish and Game documents were required to be gender neutral and fisherman became fisher.
[5] In the early 1970's most commercial fishermen still used set nets. A typical fishing site had a heavy anchor with a large buoy anchored offshore. While fishing, a 50-fathom gillnet, the legal limit, was hung from this anchored buoy to a point on shore. The salmon would then swim into the net and be caught by the gills.

fishery in Cook Inlet while I was assisting him placing the test fish nets. Getting my first experience with a gill net. Based on Reardon's explanation I asked Charlie a question I already knew the answer to; "Charlie is the fish camp on your allotment?[6]

"No." he answered puzzled.

"Do you have a permit or lease from US Fish and Wildlife or Bureau of Land Management?[7]

"No. Don't need permit. Do I?" *Hasn't been watching Treasure of the Sierra Madras.*

"I'm sorry but you don't have any legal ownership of your fish camp. So, we can't throw someone off. It's first come gets the spot."

"Fish camp mine. I first. Cannot take. You throw them off. It's mine. How I pay bills.

How get subsistence fish?"

God, I really feel for this guy. What can I do. **Nothing. Remember Reardon. Cook Inlet everyone has a lease. Here just past practice.** Putting my hand gently on his shoulder to stop him from standing, "Charlie here on the Yukon everyone knows whose camp is whose. These new people from Unalakleet don't know whose camp is whose. This is their first year, I remember when they bought their licenses." *Wow! Remember the woman! The only woman who*
bought a license. She was magnificent. Perfect face. Never seen hair that black. That body! Five feet eight inches but some curves never seen before[8]. **Charlie has a problem.** *Forget her she's taken.* No wonder poor Charlie didn't challenge those guys; anyone of the three guys could have taken me. Probably the woman. *I wish.* "Do you know any elders that might be able to explain to them that's it's your camp?"

Charlie's head was hanging. "No, no. If you no help, I not know what do."

---

[6] Alaska natives had been excluded from homesteading by their race. One of the first efforts to correct this injustice had been the native allotment program which allowed people to claim forty unoccupied acres.

[7] At that time the Yukon Delta was primarily owned by either the USFWS or BLM. They issued leases for various activities. Leases for commercial/subsistence fishing camps were unknown. The local residents were allowed free access.

[8] Meet Cisco, the third companion in my head.

Shit, hope he doesn't start crying. <u>*Wonder if I went out there if I could bluff them off?*</u> *Nah, that would be illegal.* **If it got back to Geiger.** *Anyway, don't think that bunch would bluff. It's a big river must be somewhere else he can fish.*

Charlie was staring a hole though the table. "How pay bills? Feed family?"

I could walk under a worm without ducking. Got to try something. "Charlie, there must be another place you can fish."

"No. No place else left."

I stood up, grabbed the table and pulled it out from the wall, past a surprised Charlie. Who stood staring a little bewildered. The wall behind the table was papered with a set of USGS inch to the mile topographic maps. Blanchard and I had fit them together so the whole Yukon Delta was detailed on the wall. "Where is your fish camp?" I gestured to the wall with my hand.

Shaking his head, no, Charlie said "Don'[9] know. Never saw before."

Never seen a map? Wonder how they navigate. "Charlie this is Emmonak." I pointed to the map. "Do you go upstream or downstream to your fish camp?"

Charlie watched my hand point up and down the Kwiguk[10] Pass. "That way." He said pointing.

"Ok, you would come out on the main river here." I traced a line with my finger. "Where do I go now?"

Charlie's face brightened, he stepped to the wall and began tracing a line from my finger downstream quite away. Muttering in Yup'ik. *Probably naming places as he recognizes them on the map. He picked this right up.*

"There fish camp." He pointed to a small peninsula sticking out into the river.

"Ok. I'll mark that." I picked up a pen from our Blazo box shelves[11] next to the radio and made a dot. Then wrote, Charlies Fish Camp.

---

[9] On the Delta most people don't pronounce the "t" in don't. Not quite sure how to reproduce it phonetically. Most of us newbies picked it right up in our own speech.

[10] Yup'ik for leak, I was told. Which fits since it's a distributary taking some of the Yukon's water to the Bering Sea.

[11] Blazo, Chevron's brand name for white gas, came in twin five-gallon cans packed in wooden boxes. The boxes seemed to be ubiquitous in Alaska and were the shelf of choice from dorm rooms to fish camps.

"You make leave now? That official." *Shit, he doesn't get it. Just keep on with plan.*

"No, but let's see if we can find you just as good a spot." **You don't know anything about picking a fishing site.** *Yeah, but he does.* "If we go downstream"

"No good downstream too far."

Well, that takes care of downstream. "Ok, how about here?" I pointed to the next point of land upstream.

"No good. To shallow."

"How about here then?" I said moving upstream to the next point, which was across the river.

"No, that's Sameroff fish camp."

"Would he let you fish there too?" I asked.

"No, no he has three boy. They all fish. No room more net."

"Ok. How about this point?" I continued choosing protrusions, large and small, moving back upstream towards Emmo. Each one was already someone else's fish camp or it was too shallow, to many snags, river was too fast. Each suggestion was shot down. *Charlie work with me. You're the fishermen. I don't know what I'm doing. Probably should have written down all those fish camps.*

"How about here?" I said trying to keep the frustration out of my voice.

"Na…" Charlie's automatic no died as it came out. He became thoughtful. Almost to himself he said quietly "Close, won't need camp. Good net site. Build drying racks and smokehouse home. Why nobody there." He thought awhile. "It work! Not good like fish camp. I try. You make Unalakleet people move there?"

"Ugh, err, no can't throw them off. But you said that spot would work. You could use it." I pointed out.

"I go see." He turned and left with the step of a man on a mission.

Hope I helped. Crap, now who is this? I sold another license and forgot Charlie.

The king salmon harvest guideline was taken in with the shortest number of fishing periods on record for the Yukon. Blanchard had left, his replacement Gary and I were the least popular people in the village due to the closure. With the fishery closed there wasn't much to do. Except listen to people grip. Gary was walking off listening to a mornings grips. I was prefilling out chum salmon A-W-L forms for the upcoming chum salmon season. Charlie burst into the office and as I stood, he wrapped his arms around me. I recoiled in surprise and shock, men didn't hug men in the Francisco family.

"Thank you, thank you. I had the best fishing ever! Paid all my bill. Still had money.

Ordered motorcycle, new outboard! Thank you. I tell everyone you only Fishgame know fish.

Thank you."

Charlie's effusive affection was making me uncomfortable. He still had me locked in a bear hug. The familiar odor of booze coming from him. *Wow, heard there was a bootlegger in town. Guess some of Charlie's new-found wealth went to him. Happy I could help. He's sure happy with me. Won't hurt my rep in the village. Hope it gets back to Irene. Wish he would let go.*

"Charlie that's wonderful. I didn't really do anything, you picked the spot and caught the fish." I said stepping back and peeling him off me.

He immediately grabbed me again, hugging me for all he was worth. "No, you showed where fish. Guys stole fish camp, not catch fish. You know fish."

I peeled Charlie off me again. "Okay, do you want a cup of coffee?" I stepped back and walked to the kitchen for a spare cup.

"No, no. Plenty drink. You drink?"

"Thanks, but I'm on duty, can't drink right now."

"Stone-face gone. He not know."

"Stone-face", must mean Geiger. Didn't know that was his nick name. Wonder if I should tell him. **Probably not!**

"Come, we get drink." Charlie started unsteadily for the still open door. I walked beside him to the door. "Charlie you go ahead and celebrate. I have to work. I'm sure glad your season was great for you. You might want to save a little money in case next year's not so good." He wobbled happily down the ramp, waving and heading back into town. He said something in Yup'ik that I didn't recognize.

The next day, I was sitting after breakfast with a cup of coffee. KNOM blasting rock and roll over the radio as I read a book. *What was that.*

Extra beats. No, that's a tiny knock at the door. Irene! I jumped to my feet and raced to the door. Opened it with anticipation, which turned to disappointment and puzzlement. A tiny Yup'ik women stood there shyly looking at the ground.

She was maybe four feet ten, probably shorter. A very slender build with long black hair.

Wonder what she looks like? She'll look at me sooner or later. I stepped back opening the door.

"Come in. How can I help you?" I said in a quiet voice, I didn't want to scare her. She seemed like a deer ready to flee at any sound. Without looking up she walked quietly into the office. I followed, leaving plenty of space so she wouldn't be frightened. When we reached the office, I stepped around her and pulled a chair out from the table. "Please have a seat. Would you like tea or coffee?" She finally looked at me. Couldn't decide what was on her care worn face. She sat in a chair she pulled out for herself. *Guess I picked the wrong chair.*

All most inaudibly she said "Café." *That mispronunciation of coffee so many Yup'iks use is really classy. Sounds French.* I returned from the kitchen with a fresh cup, clean spoon, a paper towel and a can of condensed milk which I set before her. The spoon on the paper towel. *Make your Grandmother proud.* I filled her cup from the pot staying warm on the heater. As I sat I looked the table over. *Pretty good. First woman whose sat here. She hasn't told me who she is or why she's here. Have to ask. Irene said direct questions are impolite. How do I find out without asking?*

My guest added a lot of milk and sugar to her café', stirred and sipped. When she set the cup down I broke the silence "Hi I'm Kim." *That was brilliant, stupid.*

The tiny voice spoke to the café' "Charlie's wife."

How do I address her Mrs. Charlie? "It's nice to meet you. Charlie was here yesterday.

Hope that's not impolite. See what Dr. McClean[12] met about this indirect speech being tough.

---

[12] Dr. McClean was a professor at the University. His wife was Inuit. While she was away working on her PhD her mother came to take care of the children. He started most of the classes during that period with another story about his miscommunication with his mother-in-law.

We sat drinking coffee in silence, I had turned the radio down. *Nice fellowship, I guess. I didn't rudely ask how I could help. Should I try again. Read and wait. Charlie's good season!*

"Yes, Charlie was very pleased with his king season."

The coffee cup was still her focus, "Yes, lots money." There was a long silence. *Guess I'm supposed to say something.* Which she broke "Charlie buy much hooch." She sounded very disapproving.

Yes, he had a snoot full when he was here. Does she expect me to stop his drinking? "I'll tell him next time he's in."

Alarmed, she almost looked at me "No, no." "I won't." *What does she want.*

"You tell Charlie save money." She looked very uncomfortable.

She thinks it's to direct and rude. How do I set her at ease?

"Yes, I did." *Yep, just a brief parting remark. Surprised Charlie told her or even heard.*

"Thought it would be a good idea. So, he would have money latter."

"How save money?"

"Put it in the bank. The bank even pays you for putting it there."

Surprised she said "They do?"

"Yes, it's called paying interest."

"Why pay?"

"The bank puts everyone's money together and then they lend it to people. They charge the person who borrows interest until they pay the bank back. Then they keep part of the interest and give part to the people who put money in the bank."

Mrs. Charlie finally looked at me "Why?"

Wow, no experience or knowledge of banks. No bank in Emmonak, no wonder. Where do I go from here?

"It's like saving fish for winter. If you had 100 extra dried fish you didn't need but your neighbor did you would loan them to him. When you loaned him the fish he agreed to give you back a 110-dried fish at the end of the next fishing season. That extra ten dried fish would be the interest."

"If need fish just give."

"Of course, you would, because they are your neighbor and you're a good Christian." Mrs. Charlie beamed. *Guess that it the right cord.*

"The bank is different because they deal in money not dried fish. They take everyone's money not just their friends. You would take your extra money to a bank. They would give you a receipt." *Looks confused, need my checkbook, which is overdrawn. She won't know.* I quickly got up and retrieved my checkbook. Mrs. Charlie was studying her coffee when I came back.

"Like this." I pulled my last deposit receipt out. *Lucky, I didn't throw that away.* "When everyone with extra money puts it in bank, the bank ends up with a lot of money. They always keep some so if you write a check, they can pay who you wrote the check too. If you have a check book, like mine, you could write a check for ten dollars and get ten dollars. Or you could write a check at the store to pay for groceries. You keep track in this part of the check book so you always know how much money you have left to spend. *Unless you copy the last check into the balance, like you did stupid.* If you need a lot of money, more than you have, to buy an outboard or something. Then you can go to the bank and get a loan. Then you send them a check every month for a small amount until you've paid it all back. But to pay the people with money in the bank, the bank charges you interest. So, the outboard costs a little more." *Did she go far enough in school to know checkbook math?*

Recognition lite up her face. "Like charging at AC."

"Yes, AC is kind of a bank. When you charge they are loaning you the money to buy. Then when you pay it back they add interest to make money on the money they loaned you to buy." Mrs. Charlie nodded her head in the affirmative. "Give bank money. Make money like AC." "Yes, that's how it works." *She gets it, I think.*

"How keep Charlie's money, he can't give bootlegger."

Poor Charlie. But it's better for him and his family. I hope. "Next time you go to Bethel you take the money to the bank. You give them the money and open a checking account. Only the person whose name is on the check, can write a check. Like my name here, Richard Kim Francisco, can write a check and cash it to get money. If your name is on the checks Charlie will have to get money from you. But it is Charlie's money too, so you should share with him."

"Yes, yes. Like dried fish. Just use what need. Leave rest. Bank safe? Why bank not take money?"

"There are laws and special government people who watch the banks. If the bank takes money not theirs, they are punished."

"What bank robbed? Like movies?"

"The banks have to buy insurance from the government. If they get robbed insurance gives them the money back."

"That why catch robbers?"

Realization or question. "Yes, that's why we pay police. More café'?"

I reached back for the coffee pot on the heater and warmed-up our coffees. *Need a break.*

This making sure to always use subjects is tough. Never realized all understood subjects I used.

Mrs. Charlie forgot to add sugar or cream. With a furrowed brow she looked at my checkbook.

Should I say something. She's thinking. Better leave her alone. Will she notice I'm overdrawn? After what seemed like a long time, since I was a little uncomfortable about robbing Charlie, she asked "How get check book?"

"If you go to bank in Bethel, be sure you go to the bank, don't get a checkbook from anyone else. Tell them you want a checkbook. Someone there will help. In Bethel they probably have someone who speaks Yup'ik who can help."

"Thank you." She got up and left.

That was interesting. Hope I did the right thing.

Charlie dropped by a couple of weeks later. He was on a new Honda 50cc motor scooter.

That's a relief, I was afraid someone had sold him a Hog.

"You like motorcycle?"

"Yes, that's a nice one. My brother has one like it." I answered. Charlie started to tip over and I grabbed the bike to steady him. With our faces close, I could smell the whiskey. *Guess he kept his money.* "How's chum season going?"

"Spot you show, good for chums. Thought no more fish after king. Money gone. Had too fish. Watch go." Charlie worked the gear shift with his toe and took off in first gear. *Shift Charlie, give the engine a break.* He disappeared past the AC store. I turned to go inside but heard the whining overloaded engine coming back. Had to jump out of the way to avoid getting knocked down by Charlie. He managed to stop, started to tip over. I saved him again. *His pants are a filthy wreck. Guess he tips over everywhere he stops.*

"It go fast."

It would go faster if you shifted but I'm not showing you. Dangerous enough in first.

"You want drink?"

"No thankyou Charlie I'm working."

"OK, see you." Off he went, full throttle, first gear, the poor abused scooter crying out in agony. *Wonder if the tranny or engine will blow first.*

❦

A year had passed and I was back in Emmo for my second summer as a fish ticket editor and "other duties as assigned."[13] The agonized whine, that had become familiar by the end of last summer, met my ears. I instinctively stepped aside; First Gear Charlie passed by me heading uptown. *Amazing, Honda should be proud, engine and tranny still working after a year in first gear at full throttle.* I waved, but Charlie didn't seem to notice. Continuing on towards the sauna and shower I was over taken by a group of boisterous Yup'ik children. To avoid stepping on a child, I stopped, as I started again I heard a woman's voice say "Hello." Turning I saw the tiny Mrs. Charlie smiling at me. "Camai" I said using up fifty percent of my Yup'ik (the other half is doy).

She came up to me then staring at the ground said quietly "I hide money. Go to Bethel for well mother check." *The new baby, in that chest carrier.* "People at bank nice. Give checkbook, tell how use. Give Charlie little money; bootlegger, gas. He happy. Plenty money. Family happy. Thank you. You help. I go Coop. Cash Charlie check. Doy."

"I'm happy for you. If you have any questions stop by. Congratulations on the new baby."

---

[13] A phrase included in most of ADF&G's job descriptions. You never knew what you might be asked to do.

Wow, meddling really helped. Feels good. Wonder if she thought of Charlie's allowance on her own or if they suggested it at the bank. Looks like she has a new dress. New baby, they must still be happily married.

She looked up at me, quickly smiled, then quickly followed the children up the road.

THE SKIFF

One, Two, Three I swung the tiller of the outboard hard over to starboard (right for you lubbers) and the bow of the wooden plank skiff responded, swinging into the oncoming wave then climbing violently up, as the huge fourth wave rose up like a wall. As the skiff crested the wave, I made a small adjustment in the tiller to port so the skiff slid down, quartering the back of the wave returning to my course. In my head, my regular companion, Kim, once again resuming the monotonous wave count. *one, two, three; swing, one, two, three, swing.* On the quick ride down the back of the waves I tried to remember the physics of waves. But the need to count always interrupted. *Why this pattern, three large followed by a huge, roll your boat over and capsize it wave. One, two, three, swing. One, two,* CRACK, COLD, *blind, under water, going to drown.* My head emerged from the wave, automatically my left hand came up to straighten my glasses. **Take 'em off. Can't see through wet lens.** Following Richard's instructions, who always got us out of trouble, I stowed my glasses.

Two of the skiff's planks had broken along with the frame they were attached too. A fountain of water now poured into the boat through the broken planks. *Can I make Sunshine Slough? To hell with meeting waves. The boat was afloat.* **GET AS CLOSE AS YOU CAN BEFORE THE BOAT SINKS!**

Full throttle raised the bow causing the water in the boat to come back around my legs and waist. Water poured over the transom and back into the river. The bow was so high I couldn't see past it but it raised the hole above the water. Water still shot in when waves hit. *Would the boat hold together until we reached shore?* **Your afloat. Worst of leaks fixed. Bail. Don't panic.**

My left hand was busy keeping valuable flotsam like the gas cans in the boat as they bobbed around me in the flow of water pouring over the transom. The bailer, a one-gallon plastic jug, cut into a scoop came to hand. My left hand and bailer started double duty, bailing as quickly as possible and pushing flotsam back into the boat. Finally, the top of the transom appeared out of the water. *Only need to bail now.* The bow was so high that the hole was still out of the water. I ignored seamanship or perhaps I was demonstrating perfect seamanship? I maintained the highest throttle necessary to keep the hole out of the water. Which was too fast for the conditions. Every wave slammed the boat, flexing and breaking more of the planks attached to the broken frame. Further opening the seams in the old wooden boat whose maintenance had been neglected so many years.

Was my rush to shore the best plan? Would the boat break into pieces before I got there?

Then the bow began to drop and I had to back off on the throttle to maintain a stern low position in the water. I was in the wind shadow of the shore surrounding Sunshine Slough now. The smoother water allowed the boat to go faster as it attempted to rise on to the step. My nearly blind aim had been good, I was headed straight into the slough.

The Bering Trader is on downstream shore. If you have to walk, ground on that shore All the seams on the starboard side were leaking, seemingly from bow to stern. A second frame had broken. The hole grew and water filled the boat faster than the left arm could bail. Even at full throttle outboard no longer could lift the bow. I aimed for the downstream shore of the slough. The transom was nearly awash again. The water was but to my butt. We weren't going to make shore.

Most valuable thing in the boat is the outboard. *Or me?* I reached into the cold, brown water covering the transom, found the mounting bolts and turning the handles to loosen them.

The boat slowly settled to the bottom. Like I knew what I was doing as the outboard's skeg hit bottom, I shifted to neutral and stood up, an idling motor in my hands but out of the water. I thumbed the kill switch then stepped out of the boat and waded ashore. The gas can, attached by its fuel line, followed like a toddler's pull toy. *Dad would have liked my new pull toy. No noise maker to take out.*

A quick glace found only a little piece of the bow showing where the skiff had sunk. A spare gas tank, a seat cushion/life preserver and the oar floated around marking the location. **STOP; sit, think, observe, plan.** *Rules of survival.* **Better collect floating gear first.** It took wading out to the sunken boat several times to gather all the floating gear. On the last trip I went to the tangled mess of floating polypropylene anchor line marking where the anchor rested on the bottom of the sunken boat. *Only about ten feet from shore. Pretty good with a sinking boat.* <u>*Dumb shit. You ended your career before it started.*</u> I gloomily reached in to the water for the anchor. **Mark boat location.** Forgetting the anchor, it wasn't going anywhere. I found the ends of the anchor and bow lines, I joined them with a square knot. *Never know when Boy Scouts will come in handy or was it Cub Scouts?* Reaching into the cold water past my shoulder I found the anchor and wadded to shore. Untying the anchor, I added it to my collection of gear. Then performed what I believed to be my final act of responsibility, I tied it to the largest willow tree it would reach. It was only two inches in diameter but was bigger than most of the willow whips growing there. I had saved everything, but the boat. <u>*Except your career as a Wildlife or Fisheries Biologist. I hate you.*</u>

I sat down on a cushion, struggling out of calf high rubber boots. <u>*Damn wet boots. Seal so tight suction won't let go. Finally!*</u> I poured the water out. Put the wet boots back on. *Find out if wool really is warm when wet. Glad I spent the money for Helly Hanson Commercial grade rainwear. Body and legs wet but warm. My hands are freezing in this wind. Gloves? In coat pockets, rubberized cotton gloves. Help a little.*

Boy Scout, Hunter Ed class and the survival manual by Rae Baxter[14] all kicked in: *Second phase of STOP, Shelter is first. The rain gear, wool halibut jacket and pants seem to be keeping me warm. Satisfactory shelter for now. Leave weaving a wickiup out of willows on the shelf for now. Ten gallons of gas, matches for my pipe, will take care of fire when I need it. Burn wet willows, tough! No one can get to Bering Trader without going past. Sooner or later someone would stop. How long until the wind let's anyone travel? Plan for now. Completed STOP for now. Wait for help, for hour. Then walk to Trader.*

My career as a Wildlife or Fisheries biologist was over. They would never forgive losing a boat! The folks at Green liked my work. I can change majors to business and work for them.

<u>*Really not fair. You told Geiger this boat had dry rot when I first got it ready for the season.*</u>

---

[14] Rae was a fisheries biologist in the Kuskokwim Area who had written a very practical survival manual that we had been given in orientation.

You have to maintain wooden boats. Can't just use and turn em upside down all winter until the next season. Considering Comm. Fish got it from FWS[15] with statehood the poor thing is at least 15 years old. Who knows how long the Feds mistreated it before that. Pretty damn well-built boat. Crying shame no one ever took the time to maintain it. It could have been beautiful with a polished wood finish instead of painted green with house paint.

The sound of an outboard motor interrupted my self-pitying reverie. Looking through my water marked lens in my glasses, I could see a boat coming in fast from the river which appeared much calmer now. Waving my arms over my head the boat turned my way. Neatly avoided the sunken boat, nudging into the shore.

"Hi I'm Kim. My boat sank and I'm stranded here." *That was a brilliant statement of the obvious. Give me a break!* "Can you give me a ride back to Emmonak?"

"Get in." said a rain gear hood that mostly hid everything but the smile on the brown face. "I stop Bering Trader."

"Great that was where I was going. Can I load my gear now or stop on the way back?" *"That's a little presumptive."*

"Put in now."

"Thanks"

He held the boat firmly against the bank idling in gear. I carried the state's twenty-five horse and the other odds and ends out into the water alongside his boat. There was plenty of room in his "fish hold". To keep fish from sliding back around his seat or up into the bow he had added plywood walls to the boat's frames ahead of his seat and the back of the bow passenger seat.

This created an open space, the net picker on the forward seat could drop the salmon into as they were removed from the net. There weren't any fish on board now, just scales stuck to sides and bottom from yesterday's commercial opening.

The Bering Trader was a black hulled ship, about 100 feet in length. It had a low white superstructure. Inside the superstructure were bunks, galley and offices for the non-local part of the cannery crew.

---

[15] United States Fish and Wildlife Service who had been primarily responsible for resource management during Alaska's territorial days, the transfer to the State of Alaska had been about thirteen years earlier.

The actual cannery was inside the hull. I had received a tour on my first visit of the season. A line where workers gilled, gutted and washed salmon on the second deck. After cleaning, the fish were slid to workers at the next station in the line who cut the fish into steaks about a half inch thick. The steak was then halved at the next station. The halves were then passed to workers who stuffed cans full. The cans were checked on a scale for weight at the next station on the line, pieces of salmon were removed or added until the weight was right. The cans were put on a conveyor belt and continued to the capping machine which sealed the top. They then were placed on and in, there were guards on the side to keep the cans from falling off, a belt that dived below deck to the next lower deck with a defending rattle. Workers filled rolling racks, six feet high with the sealed cans of salmon. The racks were walked into the retort. When full it was sealed and filled with steam cooking the salmon.

On my first tour I was surprised that the salmon pieces included bones when stuffed into the cans. I had never noticed bones in canned salmon. I was assured the high-pressure cooking in the retorts "dissolved" the bones. No doubt adding calcium to a healthy meal.

John[16], my rescuer, I learned his name on our short trip to the Trader, picked up cash for fish delivered the day before from the bookkeeper. He turned down the offered check. The same bookkeeper gave me the state's yellow copy of the previous day's "fish tickets". They are preprinted receipts with spaces to record the number and weight of the five species of salmon. There are three pages, the second and third separated by carbon paper. The white original was filled out and given to the fisher. The second yellow copy went to the state (me in this case) and a third pink copy for the buyer's records.

"The boat sunk, John rescued me from the shore, so I don't know how I'll be able to get here after the next period. I'll give you a shout on the radio when I know." I explained to Al[17] the bookkeeper.

"Sounds like you had an exciting morning. I stay safe on the Trader. Can't swim, afraid of water. Let me know if I should find someone headed that way to drop off next period's tickets." Al replied.

---

[16] My apologies to my true rescuer. I have forgotten your name but you still have my thanks.

[17] Again, my memory failed me. So, I made up a name.

"Thanks. We'll work something out." ***Don't think Geiger will want tickets entrusted to just anyone. Warned they were confidential.*** John was already out the door and headed back to his boat. Stepping to the door I said "Guess we're leaving, see you soon." *If I still have a job.*

The fish tickets were safe inside my raingear and life preserver. The cheap vinyl briefcase Geiger had supplied to keep the paperwork dry had leaked previously. Blanchard and I got back to the office/bunkhouse and decorated it with drying wet license books, fish tickets, and other miscellaneous forms kept in the briefcase.

As we were settling into the boat and casting off I asked John why he choose cash instead of a check.

"Check isn't money. I don't want Coop or NC know I sold here. Doy"

"Why don't you want them to know you sold here?" he looked uncomfortable "I won't tell." I promised.[18]

He turned starting his outboard which pretty effectively ended conversation. Actually "Doy" had ended the conversation but I was still learning local customs. Yup'iks finished speaking, conducting business and virtually everything by saying doy. Useful since it avoided interruptions. Didn't work well on inquisitive new comers.

It was a wet trip back to Emmo, it had stopped raining but the waves were much lower, it still was a rough ride. Slipping into Kwiguk Pass was a relief since it was sheltered from the wind and the waves virtually disappeared. I had asked William Trader, our local contract net mender, what Kwiguk meant, he said "leak". Looking at a map that made sense, it was one of many channels, distributaries if you were taking a limnology test, that broke off the main river to empty into the Bering Sea. The Yukon Delta was composed of a fan formed by these channels. It's dead flat, a hill is the occasional twenty-foot sand dune. Depending on the height of the water table the Delta is either water, muskeg, native grass or alders and willows.

John dropped me and the gear off at the miserable excuse for a dock located at the Northern Commercial Offices. It barely floated with me

---

[18] I learned latter fishers bought groceries, motors, virtually everything from the stores run by the processors. Their accounts were paid from their fish sales. Selling for cash to a processor where they didn't have a charge account gave them some disposable income.

and the outboard. I piled everything on shore except the two gas tanks. I picked up John's funnel and his spare empty gas tank.

"What doing?"

"I can't pay you for the ride. No money, but I can give you this gas."

I placed the funnel into John's tank and poured the gas from one of the sunken skiff's tanks into it filling it. I then repeated with John's other spare tank.

"To much." He almost whispered. Took me a moment to grasp his comment, then I realized a trip from Emmo to the Bering Trader used about a quarter of a tank of mixed (outboard motors are two cycles so use gasoline mixed with a special oil) $2.75 a gallon gas[19]. A high price back in the early 70s but getting gas to Emmonak required a special ocean-going barge or chartered airplane.

"No, it's not enough." I took his hand shaking it. "You really bailed me out of a tough spot.

Thank you."

John smiled as we shook hands. "Sometimes river rough, tide and wind different direction.

Smoother when same direction."

"Thank you, I'll remember that. See you around."

John nodded and started his motor. I thought about what he had said. Never occurred to me to look at the tide book and wind direction. Made sense, when they were in opposition the waves would be bigger. Silly Midwest boy, I wasn't use to tides. *I'm learning. What for your history!*

I worked my butt off tallying the fish tickets and completing the dot sheet. A huge ruled pad of paper, two by three feet, per Geiger instructions each fishers name was written down the rows on the left side. The date of the fishing period across the top of the vertical rows. The result, each name had a box on the date of each fishing period. Now the fun really began. Going through the fish tickets one at a time placing a dot under each fisher's name. Most commercial fishers delivered to more than one processor, like John had done. If fishing was good they may have delivered

---

[19] Price in 1972 in Emmonak was over $2. Gas averaged 0.36 cents a gallon in the lower 48 states.

multiple times even to one processor or at that companies' tender.[20] Counting how many fishers had at least one dot told you how many fishers there had been that period.

Not everybody fished every period for reasons ranging from mechanical breakdown to one unique to western Alaska. There were a number of people still new to a cash economy. They often would fish to pay for a repair or new motor or some other bill. Once the bill was paid, they stopped fishing. The idea of accumulating more money than needed for the moment wasn't part of their mindset. As I had learned from Charlie and his wife.

It was surprisingly difficult to count the dots and get the same number twice. Especially for my dyslexic eyes. Usually at least three counts were needed. Knowing the number of fishers allowed calculating the catch per unit effort, in this case the number of salmon caught per fisher hour (number of fishers' times hours in the fishing period). This number, I would later learn, is an index of fish abundance. For example, if the CPUE was ten salmon per fisher/hour there were ten times more fish than when it was one salmon per fisher/hour.

Skipping lunch, I spent the rest of the morning and afternoon tallying the tickets and doing the dot sheet. *Missing Blanchard now. Wonder when the new guy comes. You're a fish ticket editor. If you have the results two radio schedules early maybe they'll go easy on sinking the boat. Fat chance. Thanks.*

At four thirty my dot sheet count finally agreed for the third time. Recording the number, I switched the radio over from KNOM to the state channel. Fritz was just finishing the Kuskokwim projects. A beautiful voice reported no salmon had passed the weir that day. She added they had decided the single king salmon reported yesterday was in fact a beaver. Not a salmon. *Boy wouldn't being stationed with her be nice. No lonely nights. You don't even know what she looks like, you horny collegiate. At least one woman got hired. Weir is Baxter's project. Glad it's Fritz. Rather tell him than Geiger.*

"KE6628" Flat Island, KE6628 Flat Island this is KE6628 Bethel." Geiger's voice was loud and clear.

Your fucked. I didn't hear the test fishing report from Flat Island, in the mouth of the Yukon. Trying to come-up with the right words. *A*

---

[20] Large boats sent out among the fishers with scales, fish tickets and sometimes even cash, to buy fish. Saving the fishers time, allowing more time to fish.

light-hearted approach will be best. Bethel We, no, you're alone now. I have good news and bad news. Good news is I have the fish ticket totals.

Are you ready to copy?

"KE6628 Emmonak, KE6628 Emmonak this is KE6628 Bethel calling." Interrupted my mental rehearsal.

Ugh, KE6628 Em, err, I mean Bethel this is Emmonak. I have news. *Shit screwed-up.* **Take control.** The fish ticket totals are ready. You ready to copy?" *Guess he wasn't ready. That good or bad?*

"Emmonak go ahead."

"Bethel this is Emmonak. There were 14,222 kings, 92 red, and 12,034 chum salmon. Effort was 134. Over." I said.

"Got it. Give you last word." Geiger answered, always all business.

Gee no ata boy for being early. "The bad news is the skiff sank in Sunshine Slough today." "We're you able to bail it out?" Geiger asked.

"No. The rotted frames broke and planks came off. I was lucky to get off the river. Afraid she's gone." *Here it comes.*

"Is it in a spot you can describe?" Geiger asked.

Huh? Not expecting that. "Um, yeah. I was able to tie the bowline to a willow tree on the edge of Sunshine Slough."

"Good. We can surplus it. Bethel out." Geiger summed-up my near-death experience.

"Emmonak out." *Surplus it! What about a replacement? What about me? Do you think I swam back! I don't understand.* **Be relived.** *Yea, you ain't fucked.*

I was to learn on Geiger next visit, that putting a piece of state equipment up for sale as surplus, even if the condition was "SALVAGE". Only required filling out one form. In fact, several pieces of equipment could be listed on that single form. Virtually everything the Department of Fish and Game sold as surplus was condition SALVAGE. Budget constraints required us to use everything until it was used up. Not always the most efficient or safe practice. A LOST piece of equipment, such as sunk in the Yukon River, required many more forms and sworn affidavits. If headquarters in Juneau didn't like what they saw then sometimes they would even send an investigator to determine if it was stolen.

There were no other repercussions because Geiger had noticed that the skiff's working life was at an end. He had started the process of obtaining a replacement a couple of years ago. The new aluminum skiff had arrived on the first barge in Bethel that spring. When I reported the loss, the replacement was already at the Bethel Airport waiting to be flown to Emmo. My "bad" news, wasn't really news. Just changed the location of the surplus skiff.

CANCER

The foreman of the "slime line" slid a beheaded king salmon, that had been opened from anus to head, across the table to Gary and I. "What this?" he asked.

I lifted the belly flap, interested, I turned the fish onto her back so I would have a clearer view of her guts. Separating internal organs with my finger, it became clear that one ovary was normal and filled with orange eggs. The other ovary was a hard mass of tissue. I excised it with the scalpel I was using to open king salmon vents enough to slip a finger in and feel for eggs. [21]I sliced the tube of tissue in half. It was hard tissue with layers of soft adipose but poorly developed eggs were scattered about the mass. I turned to the foreman, a middle aged Yup'ik man, saying "It's a tumor. Not a problem." I slid the fish back to him. His face was puzzled, he didn't slide the fish back to the processing crew. He didn't even touch the fish.

"What?" He asked.

"The eggs didn't develop right. Just made a lump." I tried to explain.

He shook his head no. Clearly not understanding.

Gary tried to help "Cancer."

Gary and I were suddenly alone at the head of the long table where moments before ten workers stood on each side. They were now jostling each other to get out the side door.

The workers, mostly women from the village, 18 to 65. Except for two older men who stood on either side of the table, first in line. These men were the "headers". They skillfully made a precise straight cut from the anus up the belly to the base of the head. They then beheaded the fish and passed it down the line of women to be, gutted, washed and loaded on a freezer tray that was slid into a rack on wheels. When full the rack was rolled into a walk-in freezer.

---

[21] Ocean bright king salmon can't be sexed by external morphology, requiring an internal exam.

Fish ticket editors, like Gary and I, were also responsible for sampling the commercial salmon catch for age-weight-length, always called A-W-L. We didn't actually weigh the salmon. The processors provided us with the average weight from thousands of fish on the fish tickets. A much more reliable sample for average weight. No one could ever tell me why we didn't call it age-sex-length. I've always suspected it was some biologist's Puritan streak.

Our goal was to sample 320 king salmon, 120 chum salmon and all the sockeye salmon we could find. These goals had been set by the Commercial Fisheries Division biometrician[22] in Juneau. Geiger had explained, when asked, that the king salmon sample was larger because kings returned as four, five or six years old. Include two possible sexes and it took 320 samples to determine the average age of the salmon catch was within the allowable confidence interval. The small number of age two, three and seven kings were ignored. Since it would take an enormous sample to find enough of them.

Samples collected on the spawning grounds allowed comparing the sex and age structure of the two groups. Managers, like Geiger, could see if gear selectivity was creating a problem. For example, most female king salmon returned at five years of age. Four-year-old females were virtually nonexistent while six-year-old king salmon were predominately male. Eight-inch stretch gillnets, favored by commercial and subsistence fishermen for king salmon caught predominantly five-year-old females. If the targeted king salmon fishing effort, fishermen-hours, was too great, the spawning grounds would be dominated by male kings. A predominately male spawning ground population resulted in very poor reproduction and smaller future salmon returns. Probably a lot of unsatisfied males too.

We were alone, except for a dubious foreman, who had backed against the wall.

"Oops, shouldn't have said cancer." Gary said.

"Yeah, lets stick to tumor, while we try to fix this." I decided.

The kass'ak manager appeared "What the hell is going on?"

I grabbed the tumor and walked over to meet him. "That king had an ovary that became a tumor." I held out the tumor in my hand. He

---

[22] Biometrician's are experts in statistical mathematics who specialize in problems biological.

looked but didn't take it. "The crew didn't understand tumor, we made the mistake of calling it cancer. Everyone bailed." "Shit, how do I fix this?" He said.

Think his question rhetorical. *I'll try to help.* "I'll toss the tumor in the grinder.[23] If it helps we can take the king home for supper?" *Win, Win, haven't had a king since Flat Island.* "Ok. You grind it. No, wait they might not want it in the river. They drink that water. I'll see what they want? Got to get this damn line working again." He followed the crew outside.

When the door opened I could see a huddle of yellow apron clad workers waiting.

The foreman returned "You get rid of sick fish and the tumor. Then we go back to work." "OK." Gary pushed the "sick fish" too me as I approached.

"What are you going to do with it?" he asked as I picked it up.

"Put it in the cooler in our kitchen. Fresh salmon for supper. Judging by the weight, probably breakfast and lunch too. I'll be right back."

When I returned the crew was busy cleaning fish. The foreman had found two young men to load the fish on to the table. Gary, who was Blanchard's replacement, was watching the process. It was his first sampling experience so everything was novel. **The tote of fish you were sampling is empty now. Should throw the sample sheet and scale card away. Start over.** *By the time we hit three twenty it'll be random enough. Not starting over.* **Not good science.** <u>Yeah, screw you. Good enough science for anybody.</u>[24]

"Hi, we're ready to start again." The loader's exchanged words with the foreman in Yup'ik and stepped aside returning to other tasks. We returned to the head of the line. Sampling and sending the fish on.

The need to sample for length is not obvious. Because a salmon's nose (kype) grows as it approaches the spawning grounds. We measured the mid-eye to fork of tail length to the nearest millimeter. This was done with a meter stick that had a metal pointer clamped to zero and another pointer on a plastic slide. The zero pointer went on the salmon's pupil and you

---

[23] EPA requires that the waste parts be ground into small pieces before they are returned to the river.

[24] It actually wasn't bad science. Sampling was often slower than butchering so we rarely were able to sample every salmon in a tote.

slide the other pointer to the fork of the tale. The stick avoided adding the length of the curve of the body. We also had a metric tape measure which we used on the big salmon who were over a meter long. When a scale is unreadable, the fish is aged by comparing its length to the average length for fish of known ages.

It gets to be monotonous and tiring after a while. With two of us, one kept his hands clean and recorded the data called out by the other. Who picked up the salmon, sexed, measured it and picked the scale. Gary was the newbie, so he was dirty hand man. "Why can't we pick them up by the tail? It would be easier." *Questions, thought he wanted to sample fish. Shut up, he's asking the same ones we did the first time.*

"Surprisingly, if you pick them up by the tail, even though their dead, it creates vertical "bruises" down through the meat from the spine. I didn't know that till this job and the foreman caught me tailing a fish. Traditionally, salmon anglers always tail them. Not sure what that does to the survival of the ones they release. Better restock the line, we're slowing things down.

When I get back I'm going to check if tailing them while alive causes injuries." [25]

Gary took some more fish out of the box and slide them onto the line. Then he laid one out in front of himself and picked up the meterstick.

"First sex." I said.

"Why?" Gary asked looking at me strangely.

"It's first on the data sheet." I answered.

"OK. That's simple." He picked up the scalpel instead, carefully enlarging the vent with a very small straight cut forward as instructed. If your cut isn't straight it throws off the butcher making the belly-cut. Lowering grade of the fish for the fresh frozen market and the price.

We'd get thrown out and couldn't sample.

Gary stuck his index finger into the hole and felt around.

"This is the closest you'll come to sex till you get home." Some titters from the audience at my witticism. "Not sure if its necrophilia, bestiality or homosexuality." I added.

"Are all you biologists sex maniacs?" Gary asked.

---

[25] It does.

31

"Pretty much. There wouldn't be any biology without reproduction. Here's the forceps." I said smiling.

"Their tweezers say tweezers."

"Not if you're doing science." I said.

He located the "preferred area" and pulled a scale and stuck it in his mouth.

"What not rinsing it under the hose anymore?" I asked.

He stuck the scale into the next empty numbered space on the scale card.[26] "You were right.

You have to lick it to tell which side goes up anyway. May as well clean it in your mouth.

Saves time. Why does the rough side have to go up?"

"When I asked, Geiger told me they use a heated press to put an impression of the scale on plastic. Then they put the plastic under microfiche reader so they can age fish by the rings." I explained.

"Why not just any scale?"

"All the questions I asked. Thought you were going to be an attorney not a biologist? That's where the scales start growing first so they're the oldest scales. Still might be unreadable if the scale was lost and a new one grew in to replace it. Which is why we take lengths. By comparing the lengths of fish of a known age with the ones with unreadable scales you can estimate their age. Geiger says the samples from the spawning grounds can really be hard to read since the fish often are reabsorbing the scales." I vomited most of what I knew.

"How many more?" Gary asked.

"Were only on the third sheet. We're about to finish ninety. We're not done till we get to 320 then we do 120 chums."

"We aren't quitting at five?" Gary asked.

Think he's getting bored. "Nope. Didn't you sign the slave labor form?" I asked.

"Which one was that?"

---

[26] Scale cards actually were the adhesive side of heavy brown paper shipping tape. The adhesive side is hand stamped, another dull job, with a form for a heading matching a data sheet and thirty numbered squares where you stick-on a scale that corresponds with a data line on the A-W-L sheet. A-W-L sheets for some reason had forty data lines, so ten are left blank. A mystery I never solved.

"The one that said I agree to work until the job is done and get paid for 71/2 hours a day for six days a week." I said.

"No. I don't think so. Guess Sportfish has different hiring papers." Gary postulated.

"We'll supper with our fellow slime line workers at the cafeteria when the foreman calls a break. There won't be any fish available in the morning so if it's OK with you we'll stay at it till we get the full sample size. Haven't made it yet on chums because they weren't running strong enough those first periods but I think we might make it tonight." I said, hoping to enlist him in my ambition.

"OK. It's not like I have anything else to do. Eight hundred and fifty-seven." He rattled off the next king salmon's length.

We continued our evening's entertainment. We did make our chum salmon goal for the first time that night.

SOCIAL SECURITY

"I NOT DEAD! I NOT! I NOT DEAD!" Caught completely by surprise, I spilled my coffee in my lap, closing my book without marking my place. A plump old Yup'ik woman stood at the end of the table waving a piece of paper. *Shouldn't have left the door open.* *To damn hot to leave it closed.*

"I NOT DEAD. NOT DEAD." My guest continued screaming, waving the piece of paper.

"Yes, I can see your very much alive. Could you sit down?" I said in my calmest voice.

"NOT DEAD. SAY I DEAD! I NOT DEAD! YOU SEE I ALIVE, NOT DEAD! TELL THEM NOT DEAD! I NEED MONEY!" She said still waving the paper in her hand.

"May I see the letter?"

"Yes, yes, letter." She almost handed it to me but went off again. "SAYS DEAD. I NO DEAD. I ALIVE." She began waving the letter frantically in front of my face. Her panicstricken face looking up into mine. "I ALIVE!" She pounded the letter against her chest. *She's going to tear it.* *Take a chance.* I reached out and rather firmly grabbed her wrist on the upswing. Now both of our hands were waving and beating on her chest. I didn't want to hurt her, but I increased my hold until I had control of her hand.

"May I read the letter?"

"Yes, yes read letter." But her grip on it was still like iron. As I pulled on the letter, she slowly let it slid from her fingers. "My letter. I keep."

"Yes, I will give it back as soon as I read it. Then I will know what you need to do." "YOU TELL I ALIVE!" she said loudly as I read the letterhead. She pointed at the radio. "YOU TELL I ALIVE!"

I could see the letterhead. "We can't talk to Social Security on the radio," Panic increased in her face. "but I will read letter. Then help you write one to prove your alive." *Why did you save that?* **He has a point, this isn't your job.** *Shut-up and let me read please.*

Hope there's instructions on making appeal.

There weren't any appeal instructions. The letter was pretty simple, with a few bureaucratic flourishes it said "We regret to inform you that your application for social security benefits has been denied because the applicant is deceased.

"You tell not dead?" A small scared voice said.

Her voice had dropped and was trembling. *Great now she's going to cry. Hey be nice.* "Mrs. Charles[27] I'll help you write a letter back proving your alive but I'm going to need your help." I said.

"OK." She answered.

I reached for the yellow pad under the radio I used for notes. *Think what they will want.* "What is your birthday?" She rattled off a date, without the year. "What year were you born?" I asked.

"1907"

Wow, wonder what this place was like then! She survived the flu epidemic! "Do you have a birth certificate?" I asked.

"What birth cer, ate?" She stammered trying to repeat certificate.

She doesn't know the word. Probably doesn't know what they are. Probably doesn't have one, no one here then to make them out? "It's an official letter from government saying when you were born. Maybe the priest has a record or do you have family bible with birthdates?" I was quickly running out of ideas.

"Priest no here then? No government paper." She explained.

She didn't have any tax returns, even though she worked at all kinds of jobs over the years. *How do you not file a tax return? Think of all the refunds she must have missed.* Mostly fish processors but also recently for the school as a teacher's aid. But she hadn't saved any paperwork from that job either. I finally gave up and then decided affidavits were the way to go.

Our first stop, since it was nearest, was the Roman Catholic Church. My first time since the priest stopped on his snow machine with wheels bolted to the skis (*Did that make it amphibious? Snow and ice are water.*) to invite me to services. We found him in his office doing paper-work. He knew Mrs. Charles, who upon his greeting once again launched into "I NO DEAD! TELL NOT DEAD!" refrain. I handed him the letter and he read the letter, then looked at me.

"Father, Mrs. Charles brought this letter to me and it's not really a Fish and Game problem. But I'm helping her collect affidavits as proof of life. Thought your records might have her date of birth and that you could swear too in a letter. I thought that along with postmistress and recent employer's affidavits we could straighten out this mistake." I said. "That's very kind of you. Yes, I think it would help. I'll check the parish records and write a letter. Give me a day or two. When will I see you in church?"

"I was afraid having a Lutheran in the back row might blacken your record." I said.

"We're all Christians together, your very welcome here." He encouraged me.

"Thanks, I'll think about it, no promises." I said.

"I'll have the letter in a couple of days." He said as he made a note of the address.

Once we were outside Mrs. Charles seemed a little agitated "No give letter?"

"Yes, he gave you the letter back. You have it in your hands."

"No, he not…. letter says alive." She was struggling for the English.

"He'll have it in a couple of days. He has to check the parish records to see what they say about you, so he can put it in the letter. It will take him a little time." I explained.

"OK" she said. But I could see she was concerned.

Next stop was the postmistress, who was open since a mail plane had arrived an hour or so before. She and Mrs. Charles spoke in Yup'ik as she read social security's letter. I stood behind Mrs. Charles waiting for them to finish. Finally, they both said "doy" and the postmistress asked me "What do you think I can do?"

"I thought you could write a letter on official stationary saying Mrs. Charles is known to you and has had a mail box for however long she's had one or something. Then sign it and stamp it to make it "official". I'll include it with the priest's letter and any other proof of life documents we can come up with and send it along to them." I said.

"For Fishgame you know a lot of social security." The postmistress said.

"Not really. I'm just guessing what they will want."

"OK, wait." She turned, took the one or two steps it took to get to her little desk in the back of the small building and sat down at her typewriter. Her fingers flew over the keys. *Wow she can really type!* She pulled the letter out brought it back to the counter, signed it, had me sign as a witness to her signature, then wacked her canceling stamp so it hit both our signatures. She handed me the letter.

"Thank you, this should help." I said.

"I hope so. Those people should know who alive and dead. Who they think paying is paying in?" She answered.

"Yeah, that's what surprised me too." I added. *Should I ask about income taxes?*

Naw, stick to one thing. Thanks, see you again when we mail this all to Social Security. "Let's go to the school and get one about your work." I said to Mrs. Charles.

"Nobody in school. Gone summer."

"Well, let's check." She was right and it was a wasted trip.

We had better luck at the Coop. Jake's pretty secretary, was as efficient as beautiful. *Scratch another stereotype. But she's not blond.* She quickly retrieved Mrs. Charles file, loaded a sheet of letterhead in her typewriter and quickly wrote a letter summarizing Mrs. Charles recent job history. Took it in for Jake's (the manager) signature. Signed it herself attesting to its accuracy. She returned it to me asking "Will this do?"

"Looks like an attorney did it, this is perfect. Thank you." I said.

"You're welcome, but you're actually saving me some work. Usually I get stuck replying to this kind of letter, although social security is a new one for me. Health and Social Services usually sends these incomprehensible requests. The penalty for coming home after college I guess. How can they think she is dead? Who do they think has been paying all these years?" She asked.

"My question too. Hope these letters take care of it. One thing I've learned is usually there's a form and if you don't fill out the form common sense be damned." I said. Laughing she said "You got that right. Good luck Mrs. Charles, I think Kim is going to get things straightened out for you."

As we crossed the bridge over honey bucket slough, a drainage ditch left over from construction of the airport, that had been quickly repurposed to honey bucket disposal.

Mrs. Charles said "I tired. House there." She pointed to some B.I.A. plywood houses behind the post office.

"You can go home. Loan me the letter so I can write my letter. We have big envelopes at the office the letters will fit into flat, so we don't have to fold them. When the Father's letter is done I will put them all together and mail them. I'll borrow a copier so I can give you an envelope with copies of all the letters. In case you need them again." I said.

She handed me the letter saying "You mail?"

"Yes, I'll mail."

"Doy." She walked away. *Gee her appreciation is overwhelming.* **The letter is in English. That makes it our job.** *Yeah, that's an interesting dichotomy they have in their culture.*

❧

August arrived and the fall chum season was another record. Marie and I were happily living together waiting for the Coho season and her return to college. We were sweeping the Delta back outside where it belonged when Mrs. Charles arrived at the office.

She handed me a letter and lunched into a long Yup'ik explanation to Marie.

Took them six weeks to reply! They'd probably blame the mail but the date on this letter is just four days ago. Don't see a form, what does it say. I finished reading the letter that explained Mrs. Charles had been reported dead in 1932 by the Alaska Territorial government. If this record was in error it had to be corrected by the Alaska Department of Health and Social Services, Division of Vital Statistics. *Great like they have an office in Emmonak. Who the fuck they think has been paying into her account all these years. This is the reason bureaucrats have such a fucking terrible reputation. No fucking common sense.*

"Mrs. Charles wants to know if her social security checks are going to start?" Marie asked.

"I bet she said a lot more than that. Nope, we have to send proof of life to the Alaska Division of Vital Statistics, then they have to tell social security she's alive. Then the checks will start."

"Kim that's the stupidest thing I ever heard. Who do they think has been making her social security payments all these years?" Marie repeated everyone's question.

"I know, stupidest damn thing I've ever heard of, rules are rules. I've got to figure out where I can get the address for Vital Statistics? Wonder if the city office has a list of state agencies? Are we done sweeping?" I asked.

"Yes, you're done. Go check I'll finish-up."

I bent over to kiss her, she turned her head away, "No sugar. No work, no play."

Disappointed, I said "I'll stay till it's done." *Didn't think I'd get out of my chores that easy.*

She turned back to me, "You're so easy. Here." Hands behind my head she pulled me to her lips. Then swatted me on the butt and said "Get the address?" I headed uptown. Mrs. Charles looked a little puzzled but she and Marie started in Yup'ik again, I was certain everything would be cleared-up. Dust and Mrs. Charles.

The city office was closed. Sign on the door said Alex was at a training class. I walked on to the Coop and walked in to the outer office. Jake's secretary was hard at work but stopped when she saw me.

"What's up?" She asked.

"Remember the social security lady I brought in back in June?" I said.

"Yes, Mrs. Charles, did she get her check?"

"No, social security finally answered and they won't change her status until the Alaska Division of Vital Statistics says she's alive. I need to find their address so I can resend the copies of everything." I said.

"Bet your sorry you opened this can of worms? Do worms really come in cans?" She said as an afterthought as she spun on her chair to face the book case behind her.

"I'm sorry, it's hard to prove somebody is alive. You'd think that would be simple. No, I don't think I've ever seen a can of worms except in pictures and cartoons. They usually come in waxed boxes, kind like miniature king salmon boxes." *Lived in Alaska all her life, hasn't ever seen a worm.*

Laughing, she spun back around with an Anchorage phone directory. She laid it on her desk and opened it to the blue government office pages. "You always know the strangest things. Why do they come in boxes and why pictures of them in cans?"

"You've probably never seen a worm. People sell earth worms and nightcrawlers, which are really big earth worms, for fish bait. Saves you the trouble of digging them up. You put them on a hook, cast out and the fish grab the worm and hook. Then you catch the fish. A traditional scene for paintings is a little boy with a rusty food can that he has full of worms in one hand and his fishing rod in the other."

"Here it is." She grabbed a note pad and dashed off the address in Anchorage. "Guess I missed a lot going to college in Anchorage. Thanks for explaining about worms, now I understand the cartoons a little better. Could never understand why they didn't fish with nets?"

"Growing up we always thought people who used nets were cheaters. I'm learning a lot too. Thought I'd get this at the city office but Alex is at training. You're going to be gone soon when the office closes?" I asked.

"Not soon I hope, but yes, I'm just here for the summer, why?"

"I wasn't sure who to tell Mrs. Charles to go too since we'll be gone if it takes another six weeks to get a reply." I answered.

"Teachers will be back by then, just tell her to go to the principal's office."

"Good idea, thanks. Never would have thought of that, I dreaded being called to the principal's office.

Bye" I said.

To my surprise and satisfaction, since I was a state employee, Mrs. Charles was back in just four days with a letter from Vital Statistics confirming they had received the letter and were investigating the possible error. I was lucky Marie was there because I'm not sure I could have explained to the desperate Mrs. Charles that no there wasn't a check yet.

Coho salmon season came and went as the processors closed down one by one because there weren't enough fish to make it worth staying open. Marie and I kissed goodbye on the runway with me promising to meet her in a few weeks in Seattle. As I was packing, I remembered the unfinished business with Mrs. Charles. I made sure my copy of the letter from Vital Statistics was in the front pocket of my briefcase. I would be passing through Anchorage on my way to Fairbanks, thought I would make one final effort and call *Where's that letter from Health and Social Services about Mrs. Charles? Jack pot, front pocket of brief case.* I dropped a quarter in the payphone and dialed the number.

"Vital Statistics."

"Hi my name is Kim Francisco. I'd like to speak to Sally Burns[27] about Mrs. Charles of Emmonak."

"Just a moment."

"This is Sally."

"Hi this is Kim err I used my first name in the letter Richard Francisco. Mrs. Charles of Emmonak social security number 907-27-7543[28] was reported dead. She's not and I've been trying to help her prove she is alive so she can get her social security. The last letter she received was from you. I was checking to make sure everything we sent took care of the problem."

With a friendly chuckle Sally said "Should I call you Richard or Dick?" *Love Alaska informality.* "Actually, I use my middle name Kim."

"Kim, thank you very much for all your work on this. I've been through the records and found that it's sadly a rather common problem. We solved it now but these old territorial records are still a mess. No proof of death use to be required in territorial Alaska since most villages didn't have doctors or sheriffs. They assumed if a husband reported his wife dead that she was. Unfortunately, word got out that you could get a cheap divorce by reporting your spouse dead. That information went to Social Security and as you found out, they are a little difficult to deal with. Opps, this is an active case I'm not supposed to tell you that."

"Your secrete is safe with me, I just wanted the poor woman to get her money."

"Since I've let the cat out of the bag thought you'd like to know Mr. Charles remarried so we submitted the file to the District Attorney for prosecution on bigamy. I did just hear from Social Security and they are sending a settlement check for payments missed and then the monthly payment will begin. You, young man, should destroy her social security number, its confidential. I would also like to tell you I'd be proud if you were my son. " "Err well, thanks." I took a deep breath. "I'll destroy her social. Bye"

"Bye, Bye"

Damn it what's wrong with me. Get choked up over someone thanking me for doing the right thing. Hell, I wouldn't have been able to sleep nights if

---

[27] My apologies to the kind woman at Vital Statistics but I've forgotten your real name.

[28] Guess what, I made this number up.

I had blown her off. Man, reported her as dead, what a bastard. Hope they throw the book at him. Going to be a terrible surprise after all these years. Time to try Marie again.

FIRST CLOSURE

The Virgin (pronounced Virrgin, and don't you dare use the other pronunciation.) family showed up after I had announced that the king salmon catch total had exceeded the 250,000-fish, the harvest guideline. I had announced it on the CB fishery update at 8:00 AM. Mr. Virgin, the school teacher and father, sat down for coffee and conversation trying to get information from us we didn't have. Would the commercial fishery close?

His college age son finally exploded, "Why are you keeping this a secret. We have to know so we can plan to stay or run home for a couple of days. You have no right or reason to keep this a secret. You're just messing with people's lives to mess with us. YOU'RE JUST FUCKING WITH US." He finally spat out at me, jumping to his feet, closing his fists and taking a fighter's stance.

His father jumped up between us. I sat there with a wide eyed shocked look on my face. *Fighting wasn't in the job description!*

Mr. Virgin held his hand up in a stop signal "CUT THAT OUT!" turning to me he added "You really don't know do you?"

"No, that's what we've been telling people all morning. Neither of us would keep it a secret just to fuck with people. We're just tiny little gears in this outfit and we don't make the decisions."

Taking his son by the shoulders and turning him towards the door he turned his head to me "Thanks for the coffee and information. We'll just listen in at six." They left.

Gary came out of the kitchen "Thought there was going to be a fight?"

"Me too. I was too surprised to get out of my chair. Guess he would have gotten the first punch in." I said.

"Think you could have taken him?" Gary asked.

"Don't know. After getting punched I might have been mad enough to fight. Never lost a fight but I haven't been in many, I was raised to avoid them." I replied "You never lost? You have fought?" Gary asked incredulously.

"Yep. My Dad use to referee Golden Glove fights at the Jewish Community Center in Des Moines. I use to go along, mostly for swimming lessons. I was in love with Marcia the swimming instructor. I was too young to know what to do with her but she was the first crush, I remember." *She was a babe.*

"We were talking about fighting not loving?" Gary reminded me.

"Sorry, I dream of being a lover not a fighter. Anyway, Dad got me into the beginning boxer class, forget what level that was called. I got the basic skills down blocking punches, jabbing and the various real punches with the right. Dad use practice with me. But I didn't like hitting people and hurting them. I remember the instructor finally told Dad one day that I was great at the basic skills but I wasn't mean enough to be a boxer." I told Gary.

"How'd your Dad feel about that?" Gary asked.

"He wasn't happy. Tried to tell me how I would have to learn to be mean to make it in life.

We had a long talk. Guess to Dad's credit he did let me quit but he didn't let me forget how disappointed he was. Guess that's why I played football." I filled in flashes of my past.

"That was high school?" Gary asked.

"No, yes. Football was high school boxing elementary school. We moved when I was in third grade, so first or second grade." I said.

"Those would hardly be fights, don't really count as not having lost any." Gary said.

"Sorry, that's when I learned to fight but then in later years I got pushed into some fights.

The last time was in high school. I've come close to throwing a punch a couple times in college but always managed to avoid doing it." I said.

We turned off the CB, got tired of telling people we didn't know when or if fishing would close. It was my turn to sweep and I needed to do something physical. With the office door wide open and Gary safely out of the dust filled building telling the visitors "No we don't know if it will close", I swept the building from one end to the other. As I was emptying a dust pan full of silt back onto the delta from which it came, when a Cessna 185 on floats landed in front of the office. Watching the plane turn back towards our flimsy dock we realized we had visitors so I rushed back in to get the last of the pile of dirt off the floor. Gary was already at the dock so I continued getting the chairs back down around the table. Pulling the chairs down showed there dust outlines remaining. I quickly wiped it down with a wet towel. Gave the room a quick scan, *not too bad except for the remaining dust in the air, fuck em if they can't take a joke.*

An energetic slim man popped to the top of the bank. Geiger ascended in his usual careful deliberate manner with his huge briefcase, biggest I had ever seen. Gary was helping the pilot turn the plane around and tying up. I greeted them halfway to the office.

"Hi, you may want to wait out here a couple of minutes. I just finished sweeping and the dust is still settling." I warned them.

"Hi, I'm Ron Regnart." The energetic one shook my hand, I recognized the name as Geiger's boss, the regional supervisor, as I shook his hand. *Shit, what have I done that the Regional Supervisor is here.*

"I'm Kim Francisco." He quickly released my hand spun his head around looking quickly at Geiger then back to me.

"Nice to meet you. I'm use to Delta dust. Brought my son along a couple of years ago. He had just gotten a slingshot. Went crazy looking for a rock out here. Kept trying to shoot spitballs made with silt. Didn't work." Ron said. "Good to hear you guys are keeping the place up. You're the face of the Department out here." Ron continued. *Shit what did I do to lose face.* <u>*Sunk a skiff.*</u> He said as we went up the ramp and into the dusty room. "How do you like it here? This is your first summer, right?"

"It's nice, I've been learning a lot about Yup'ik people and fisheries. Sure, isn't Wild Kingdom." I said.

Laughing Ron said "That's right. U of A has a good idea to make people do a summer in the job while they still have time to switch majors. It's not what most people expect. Have you decided if your sticking with it?"

"Yes sir, I really like it, although I wish the fishing was better." I said. *Guess I not guilty.* "Good. Yep, can't catch a salmon in the Yukon without a net. Looks like Mike's ready for you?" Ron said.

Ready! Shit, I did do something. He's just being the good cop before Mike lowers the boom. I all most sprained an ankle tuning towards Geiger. He was sitting at the table with his big three ring binder open to the top page.

"Could you read me the catch figures from yesterday's period?" Geiger said.

Whew. "Yes sir," I walked around Geiger to the radio chair and picked up the clip board with the verbals on it. While I read them off to Geiger, Gary served coffee and his made from scratch cinnamon rolls.

Regnart's roll disappeared in what appeared to be an amazing single bite.

"Those are good. Who's the baker?" Ron said.

"I'm guilty." Gary added as he brought the whole plate of rolls to the table.

Geiger was busy with the adding machine, including yesterday's totals into his catch sheet.

He then moved his chair over next to Regnart's and they huddled over binder and catch figures. Regnart sat up, looked at Geiger and said "Mike it's your fishery. What do you think you should do?"

Gary and I had pulled away into the kitchen while they huddled, thinking they wanted privacy. Geiger answered Regnart so quietly that we couldn't hear his answer.

"All right then that's what you should do. You guys don't listen to the radio or anything?" Ron asked.

"Sure, usually have KNOM from Nome on." Gary answered as he walked to the radio and turned volume up. Geiger was busy printing something on the news release pad.[29]

"Would you like warm up?" I asked "You're getting Delta hospitality down. You're not as social as the Unalakleet office though. Kind of upset Rick[30] when we dropped in last week. He and Betty, a local gal with huge tits, were still in bed. He was scared to death he was going to be fired." Ron said.

"Sounds like the same girl he's dating at the university. I don't really know them accept in passing but she does have an impressive set of headlights." I answered.

Gary embarrassed me by adding "Kim's been busy trying to get Mr. Moses's daughter into bed but I don't think he's had any luck yet. Haven't found the door locked when I've come home."

---

[29] To maintain a record of everything announced officially we had a single pad with the original of any announcements. This became part of the official record. Only cross outs were allowed. No pages could be removed.

[30] Once again I couldn't remember the culprit's real name.

Red-faced I stammered "She's a good Roman Catholic girl. We're just getting to know each other."

"Don't mess up our lease." Regnart teased as I handed him his coffee.

"Do you want to read this?" Geiger asked handing the news release clipboard to Regnart.

"Nope. Maybe these guys should proof it, they'll be reading it on the CB."

"Go ahead Kim. You usually handle the news releases." Gary added.

I rescued the clipboard from poor Geiger, who seemed a little uncertain what to do with it.

He seems so confident and in charge when he's alone. Regnart doesn't seem scary. Reading it carefully to myself I wasn't surprised to see it announced the closure of the king fishery due to the harvest guideline being exceeded.

"Everyone was expecting a closure when we announced the catch numbers so it won't be a surprise. It would be nice if we put something in about when to expect it to reopen?" I said.

Hoped that sounded constructive.

Geiger's usual expression actually changed slightly. *Thoughtful. Haven't seen that before.*

Maybe I'm just learning to read him.

"Sounds like a good idea. How about it Mike when will you reopen?" Regnart asked. *A good idea! Sounds like he's giving Geiger a test. Guess that's what supervisors do?*

There was a long pause, while we listened to "Sugar" coming in from Nome.

"Add when Flat Island is catching more chums than kings. It will reopen for small mesh gear. That's by weight not just numbers." Geiger broke the silence.

"Pulling Cunningham's trick on me there, Mike." Regnart interjected.

"What?" Geiger answered.

"Now you're getting it. Paul always says "what" then he goes silent on me, while I repeat. I thought he was going deaf until I figured out he was stalling while he thought through his answer. Now I just sit quietly until he answers." Ron said.

I had sat down and was composing a paragraph below the closure announcement explaining when it would reopen. *What's small mesh gear? Whose Paul Cunningham?* "Umm, what's small mesh gear?" I asked looking up.

"Gillnets five and one-half inches or less. It's in the book" Geiger said.

"Saw that just didn't know it was "small mesh". I tried to cover my ass.

"Small mesh gillnets catch primarily chum salmon, there is a larger surplus of chums than kings since the subsistence fishery for chums is growing smaller. Snow-machines replacing dog teams. People don't need as many chums to feed the dogs." Explained Regnart.

"Is that why people call them dogs?" Gary asked before I could.

"I think that's why the villagers call them dogs. Fisheries folks nicked named them dogs because of the big canine teeth they grow on the spawning grounds. Not sure if the villagers learned it from us or nicked named them that when they learned English." Ron answered.

"What about king harvest guidelines further up river?" I asked.

"That's the fair distribution side of harvest management." Regnart explained. "Based on the subsistence surveys and commercial catch we know what the average catch is along the river. The lower Yukon has been becoming less dependent on subsistence and more of a cash economy. The Board of Fisheries looks at all the numbers and sets the harvest guidelines at what they determine to be a fair allocation of the commercial catch between the areas on the river. While still providing enough kings for subsistence and escapement. Because of the long distances Yukon salmon migrate and the poor visibility we don't have the luxury of knowing what the escapement is until after the fishing is done. Bristol Bay and other areas of the state can see the escapement as the fishery happens so management is a lot easier." *Wow, that's what we're doing.*

"So why do you have the test fishery down at Flat Island?" Gary asked.

"Mike it's your turn." Ron said to Geiger.

Mike paused as he formulated his answer "The test fishery has been run for years. We compare the catches from year to year and how the commercial catch and escapement was in those years. Then if it's a really weak run it shows in low test fish catches and we shorten the commercial season." Geiger explained.

"Sounds complicated." Gary said.

"Show them how you do it Mike." Regnart put in.

Geiger turned the thick three ring binder on the table for us to see. "Here are all the tables of the data." He said flipping through page after page of tables filled with numbers. The first page was the only handwritten one with this year's figures. "It's easier to see on the graphs." He got to the end of the numbers where the pages were graphs of the test fishery catch, commercial catch and escapement by year. Each year getting its own line.

Stat prof wouldn't like that graph, too busy.

"This is, this year's line. Geiger pointed to the only line in pencil. "Looking pretty average.

Not high or low." Geiger added.

The door opened with all its usual creaks, squeaks and thuds, the pilot came stomping in.

"Plane's all filled up and ready to go."

"Would you like a cup of coffee first?" Regnart asked.

"Nah, just the can."

"Through the door on your right then down to the end. Open the door and the pull string for the light. It's dark in there." I said. *Interesting, the can is a can. Guess that explains pot and other slang words for toilets. Wonder why the Navy taught Dad it was a head?*

"If it's an average year why did we catch the harvest guide line so fast?" I asked the question that popped into my head.

Geiger answered by turning to another graph of fishermen effort, showing it to me and saying "A record number of fishermen this year."

I grabbed the big brief case off the floor when the pilot came out, to lighten Geiger's load.

We all trooped down to the plane.

"Thanks for the management lesson. Safe travels." I told our guests.

Geiger climbed onto the float, took the brief case and folded himself into the rear seat. He was really too tall for it. Regnart said goodbye and thanked us for the coffee. With a confident experience step walked down the float, ducked under the plane stepping over to the opposite float and into the copilot's seat. Gary and I each held the bow and stern lines from float keeping the plane next to the almost submerged dock. Three people were too much for it. The pilot hopped in and fired it up. As he accelerated out into the river we both closed our eyes, let go and turned our backs to the plane as water droplets driven hard by the prop wash slammed into us.

The unknown to us the excitement was about begin.

⁂

Ed, from Northern Commercial met us at the top of the bank, "Hi Kim, I was sent to find out about opening." He seemed apologetic.

Not fair to take advantage of our friendship. Life isn't fair. **Your learning.** *That Richard or Cisco? No answer, guess that's good supposed to show insanity if you answer yourself.*

"We're about to do a special fisheries announcement, no harm in NC knowing five minutes sooner. With the harvest guideline for kings taken it's going to close until chum season." I told Ed.

"That's what I told them. No one listens to an old man except you." Ed said.

"Thanks, *is that the right thing to say?* I would be foolish not to listen." I replied.

"You're a good kid." He patted me on the shoulder then turned as he resumed his bent over hobble so he could return to his office with the news.

"He likes you." Gary said.

"Yeah, I like him. Haven't had a grandfather for a long time and he has great stories. What a life he's lived. We better get the announcement out." I said to Gary as we climbed the ramp. Inside we changed out of our rubber boots and back into tennis shoes.

"Hey, considering your handwriting looks like a typewriter and I enjoy the radio how about you do the written one and I'll do the radio?" I suggested.

"Sounds good to me. Guess we'll get to go on a boat ride latter." Gary said.

"Yep, some reason just doing the radio isn't enough to make it official. But we need to pick up fish tickets anyway." I said as Gary went to work lining up the carbon paper and news release letterhead paper. To save a little work. I dashed off a quick copy of the "approved" news release so Gary would have one to copy while I had one to read. The familiar procedure began again. I announced on sixteen that a special fisheries announcement was coming up on channel twenty-two in five minutes. After two repeats, I switched to 22. Before the five minutes was up some Yup'ik chatter began in which the word fishgame came up a lot. At the end of the five minutes,

I was holding the mike in my hand waiting for a break in the conversations with increasing frustration. A rather angry voice walked on everyone saying something about fishgame. Another voice then walked on everyone saying in English "Shut-up so he can give the announcement." A moment of silence followed which I took to be my que, "This is Fish& Game in Emmonak with a special fisheries announcement. The commercial fishery in Districts one and two will be closed until chum salmon are the dominate catch in the test fishery. Then it will be reopened with gear restricted to five and one-half inch mesh nets. The subsistence fishery remains open until the commercial fishery reopens." Then I repeated the announcement and closed with "Fish and Game standing by."

Everyone seemed to be calling at once. I was chuckling listening to the babble. Reason finally won out and there was silence after one of the calls to us, I answered "Fish and Game back."

"Will fishing open Thursday?"

"Commercial fishing is closed until chum season. No commercial fishing on Thursday.

Subsistence fishing will be open until the chum season." I answered.

"When chum season?" Asked a new voice.

"When the test fishery shows mostly chum salmon in the catch." I repeated.

"They lousy fishermen. Still using king gear. No catch chum with king gear." Is what I picked out of several voices walking on each other.

"They kass'ak college kids, no catch fish. Use old gear. Need new gear." The number of commentators was increasing.

New gear and old gear. This is new. Wonder what they mean? I wrote a note to ask Geiger.

"Fish same place. Silted in they no catch fish. Many kings. River full kings." The criticism of the test fishery continued.

"Let him talk." Boomed the earlier voice that gave me my opening.

Great what can I say.

"Fish and Game back. The king salmon harvest guideline for District one and two has been taken. The king salmon commercial fishery is closed. Subsistence fishing is still open in Districts one and two. I don't know all the answers to your questions about the test fishery. They fish every day, every tide. They fish with both chum and king nets not just king nets.

I don't understand the question about them using old nets. I picked up some of this year's nets myself after they were repaired here in town. I see everyone else repairing nets so I don't think that makes them worthless. Fish and Game standing by." I exhausted my knowledge of the test fishery.

"I'm ready to deliver these." Gary said.

"Fishgame stupid use old cotton nets not new monofilament." Came a voice.

"Yeah, stupid, river, lots fish, bills, more, fish wrong time, lazy, not, can't, keep, fish, no shoes, need stove, gas, oil,…" the babble began once again as everyone tried to talk at once.

With the babble for a background I answered Gary, "Yeah, I'm ready to deliver news releases too. Let's wait a minute and see if this settles down into anything coherent before we go."

"OK, I'll get my book." He left for the bedroom as I left the babbling radio for the kitchen and another cup of coffee. *If I don't get a coherent question by the time this is done I'll sign off and deliver news releases.*

A voice boomed in about half way through my coffee "Quiet, shut-up I need to ask a question.

Surprised that worked.

The new voice broke the momentary silence. Is the king fishing closed?"

I should ask where have you been? Nah can't say shit like that. "This is Fish and Game Emmonak back. Yes, the king salmon fishery in Districts one and two will be closed until we announce the opening for the small mesh gear fishery. Fis" "Full, stup, fish, la,… "and the babble began again.

Gary called from the bedroom "You ready to go?"

"Yes, just as soon as I sign-off, as if anyone will be able to hear me." I told him.

"This is Fish and Game Emmonak, "mor, lot, fi." The next fishery announcement will be at the usual time five PM. Fish and Game out. Switching to sixteen."

I switched to sixteen and turned off the radios. Kicked off my slippers, stuffing my feet into my Red Ball rubber boots. *This itch between the toes is getting bad wonder what the store has for athlete's foot.*

We tacked a news release to the front door, I walked one over to Ed at NC. The CB was on and the babble seemed more organized now but it was in Yup'ik so I wasn't sure.

"Folks aren't happy." Ed said as I walked in.

"Me neither. Don't shoot the messenger." I said smiling.

"Won't shoot you. You'll just get tired of listening. That's why Geiger left." Ed explained.

"Can't be much of a surprise. It closes every year when the harvest guideline is taken." I replied.

"Early this year. Only took 3 periods." Ed reminded me.

"Oh, I asked about that, we had a record number of fishermen this year. Gary's waiting.

Camai[31]"

Gary was holding the bow into the bank with the motor idling in gear. As I pushed off, he put it in reverse, I actually made a smooth landing as I jumped in for a change. *Gary looking aft.*

No one else around to see your entry. O well when someone is watching you'll trip over the seat or something. Nice being away from the radio. Too bad the boat and motor cover up all the natural noises. But you wouldn't want to paddle a canoe that far.

"Can you give this to Jake?" I asked the guy putting things away on the Coop dock, handing him the news release.

"No, you bastard, not enough money yet! You goanna feed family? You paid, fish, no fish.

Don't give fuck about us." He replied.

Ignoring the continuing stream of insults? I stepped up onto the dock and walked up into the plant, which was dark and empty. *Hope I don't get a fish pew in the back. Make an interesting murder mystery. Better write that idea down in my notebook.* Jake was out but his pretty young assistant took the news release. She was as pleasant and friendly as ever. *Guess she gets paid if there's fishing or not too. If this thing with Irene doesn't work out, wonder if she has a boyfriend or husband.*

Gary was standing off in the river avoiding the angry worker when I returned. Gary came into the dock as soon as he saw me. I climbed in and Gary let the boat drift away so we could hear each other. The worker's tirade continued.

"Wasn't too friendly at the dock. Thought I'd wait out in the river. No black eyes I hope?" Gary asked.

---

[31] Cami another word of Yup'ik I learned. Handy since it's for greeting and parting.

"No, but I was a little worried about a fish pew in the back."

"Ouch, that would hurt, guaranteed infection too." Gary added.

"Yeah, if you didn't bleed to death. Let's see how popular we are in Sunshine Slough."

The engine roared to life and I stared down into the boat. *I don't understand. If they have caught as many fish as usual, the price is high this year, then life should be good why all the complaints. With more fishermen everyone's piece is smaller. Maybe it's the high price. Everyone wants to be a millionaire. Not that one little old guy who came in after the first period for a license, he just wanted enough money for a new snow-go cylinder. Looking at the test fish catch we should be open for chums soon. Everyone is so fixated on king salmon. Probably why there's a problem with them. Everyone wants them for subsistence and to sell. Hell Kim, this is why they pay you the big money. So, people can get mad at you.* My happy thoughts continued across the river. We passed the bow of the old wooden skiff, still tied firmly to the bank. *That boat sinking out from under me was a bad day. Sure, glad Geiger had this aluminum skiff. Gary and I sure got soaked trying to raise the wooden one. What a comedy. How many willows did we uproot with the come-a-long and that mother fucker didn't move an inch. Thought wooden boats floated after they sank.*

The Bering Trader seemed deserted. The store was closed so we went aboard but the bookkeeper's office was locked. We stuck our heads into the galley. The boss was sitting having a cup of coffee and saw us.

"Come on in and mug-up." He invited.

"Thank you." We both said grabbing heavy white ceramic mugs out of a rack next to the coffee machine. With full mugs, we sat down on either side of the boss.

"Guess you got the bad news but I brought over the official copy." I said.

"Not bad news here. That's why I'm the only one sober. Everyone else is celebrating the end of the king season. All drunk as skunks."

"We wondered where everyone was." Gary said.

"Seems like a quick drunk, just did the news release an hour or so ago on the radio." I said.

"Hey, when you announced the quota was gone last night, we cleaned up the line and started the party." The Trader's boss said.

Should I tell him it's not a quota but a harvest guideline? Naw, just semantics.

"What if there would have been another opening?" Gary asked.

"We probably would have canned a couple of drunks." "You mean canned in a can, not fired?!" asked Gary.

"You never been down there when we are canning? Ask Kim. You don't want to be hung- over and slip up. You'd be a case of one-pound talls."[32] The boss said.

"Yeah, they took me down when the line was running once Gary. There was no room on the narrow gangways. Shit between conveyor belts, cans, and the butchering line it's a ballet waiting to grab you and rip an arm off."

"Preferred your own job after that as I recall. Even with sinking boats." The boss reminded me.

"Still surprised you're not as pissed as everyone else." I said.

"Fishermen are unhappy of course, they like the money. But we only have room for so many cans and we were already using cans we should have put silvers in. May miss another silver season this year depending on the chums." The boss explained.

Gary asked "Why don't you bring more cans?"

"They're about the biggest expense we have so we try to keep to what we think we can fill.

Not sure why but we got more kings than usual this year."

"Thanks for the coffee. We also came for the fish tickets, if their ready." I said.

"They're supposed to be, come with me." We all got up putting our mugs in the sink and following the boss to the bookkeeper's door. He unlocked it and picked-up the yellow fish tickets resting on the corner of the desk. Handing them to me. "Is this them?" He asked.

"Yep, thanks. Guess we'll be going." I said.

"We'll be listening for the chum opening announcement. Don't suppose you know when that might be." He replied.

"When the chums in the test fish catch are worth more than the kings." I answered.

"Guess I'll have to get up for Flat Island at seven." "No secrets on the Delta." I replied.

---

[32] The Trader was mainly canning one-pound cans of salmon but they were small diameter tall cans rather than the short wide cans.

"Not on the radio." He said.

Out in the skiff as we were leaving we saw the bookkeeper come weaving out of the deck house. He nearly went over the rail, regained his balance, unzipped his pants and took a leak over the side.

"He should stick to the inside john when he's in that condition." Gary said.

"Shit, look at him now is he going to make it." The bookkeeper instead of going back in was staggering down a narrow gangway on the outside of the ship. He almost fell in three or four times before finally reaching the boardwalk on the shore. Gary hit the throttle and we headed for Emmonak.

Ralph[33], the city manager, was waiting at the office. "Hi, Kim, would you please come to a public meeting with the fishermen to explain the king salmon closure?"

Shit, I owe Ralph one since he had that info on GED for Irene. Explain what? The harvest guideline is taken and it's closed. Guess a public meeting falls under getting the information out. "Sure, is there a time and a place yet?" I said.

"Yes, this afternoon at one, right over there in front of the NC store. I will translate for you."

"Good that should help clear things up for the none English speakers." I pulled back my coat sleeve, watch said 11:30. "Guess I better eat lunch. Camai." I said to Ralph's departing back.

Guess he has things to do and people to see.

"Sure, glad you've been here longer than me. A public meeting, sure it won't be a public lynching?" Gary said.

"Thanks, you're a big help." I said.

"I am, I'll make lunch. How's fried spam for lunch?" Gary replied.

"Think we've had that before. But if you're cooking great. I need to get a clipboard ready with what I might need. Never done a public meeting, what do I need?"

"Whip and chair might help. Pistol for sure." Gary said opening a SPAM can.

"Always fucking helpful aren't you. Wonder if the speech prof's idea of imagining the audience naked would work? Imagining girls naked always

---

[33] His name may have been Alex.

gets me tongue tied, not sure how a bunch of naked fishermen will affect me? Guess this is why Speech is a required course."

As he sliced spam and dropped it in a hot pan Gary said "You'll do fine?"

That helps. Guess public speaking is part of the job. When do I use the biology? Hard to imagine Geiger speaking in public. He seems so shy. Let's see, copy of the news release, these are those regulation proposal forms Geiger said we would never need, better take some of them. Regulation book. Should I take the commercial license forms. Nah, everyone has their license by now. Doesn't seem like much but it's all I can think of. I turned back towards the kitchen.

"Guess I have it all. Need help with lunch."

"Nope, spam's ready. Do you want to wait for toast?" Gary offered to expand the menu.

"No, breakfast seems to be sticking with me today. I'll just eat carnivore." Fresh coffee, a plate of hot spam, and my mind trying to imagine what was about to happen. Spam gone, dish in sink and I packed my pipe to smoke with a cup of coffee.

"I'm not sure which is going to kill you; all the coffee or that terrible tobacco you smoke." Gary commented.

"Kipling said "A woman is only a woman but a cigar is a good smoke."

"What the hell does that mean?" Gary asked sitting down with his book.

"Fuck, if I know but it sounds wise. It is relaxing on the nerves." "Sex is a lot more relaxing." Gary commented.

"That's not an option, unless you're up for a quickie." I replied.

"Sleeping with my back to the wall tonight." Gary said.

I took a final deep swallow of smoke, guiding it up through my nose and sinuses so the maximum amount of nicotine would enter my blood steam. The narcotic calm filled my mind as I exhaled. "Wish me luck?"

"Break a leg."

Odd expression for luck. Guess actors must give each other friendly grief the way guys do.

Ruth never understood that. Guess when women do it to each other its serious. Cat fighting?

Better shift gears. Wow, look at the crowd. They're still coming. Look at the boats on the river and people walking in from every direction. Wonder where Ralph is? Walk around the edge of the crowd to the riverside maybe he'll be there.

Suddenly two of the fishermen stepped out of the edge facing each other and making a door way for me.

"Camai" I greeted them both, smiling. Their countenance didn't change, one said something in Yup'ik that seemed to have a ripple affect opening a pathway in the crowd to Ralph, in the center.

"Hi, are you ready?" Ralph greeted me.

"Yes, thought I would be early, guess we aren't using Delta time?" I tried to lighten the mood.

"No, this is really important. Everyone is on time and ready to listen. I will stand here next to you and translate. Only say one or two sentences at a time. Then if they ask questions in Yup'ik I will translate for you. OK." Ralph gave me my stage directions.

"Yes, thank you for doing the translation. What about the people our backs are to?" I said noticing the crowd extended to the riverbank behind us.

"It's OK, they can move if they want to hear or see better. Shall we start?" Ralph asked.

"Sure." *Almost said OK again. Mix it up a bit.*

Ralph took a couple of steps in front of me then began an opening statement in Yup'ik.

Wonder what he's saying. Going to have to work on my Yup'ik with Irene. Be a good reason to spend more time with her. There was fishgame, no Yup'ik for that. Give us something to do since we don't neck yet. There's my name. Guess he's ignoring Yup'ik politeness. Irene said it's not polite to use someone's name except when talking to them.

Ralph took a couple steps forward, turned and faced me "The river is still full of king salmon yet the fishing is closed. How can we get it opened again?" Then he stepped back to my side.

Think. Obvious. Regulation book and Board of Fish and Game.[34] "The Alaska Board of Fish and Game set the king salmon harvest guideline at 250,000." Ralph gave me a stop sign with his hand. Repeated what I had said in Yup'ik. At least I thought so since I heard Alaska Board Fish

---

[34] A few years later, due to the increasing work load on the volunteer members of the Board of Fish and Game, the legislature created a Board of Fish and a Board of Game.

Game and 250,000. But he seemed to say a lot more than I had. In my next sentence I repeated the total catch and the number of kings over the harvest guideline they had been allowed to catch. Ralph continued his translation at my side. I gave the page number in the regulation book that had the Yukon River Management Plan that the Board of Fish and Game had adopted. Ralph began translating. *That was stupid, there are people who need a translator to understand what I'm saying what would the regulation book mean. The proposal forms, then we're out of here.*

Ralph had stopped and was looking up at me. "I have Board of Fish and Game proposal forms here." I said holding one up. "Anyone can fill one out and submit it. If the Board likes it they change the regulation." Stop for translation. "Mr. Geiger has told me a single proposal from a large number of people, organizations, businesses and your advisory committee would be better than just a single person's." Ralph was signaling for a time out.

He translated what I had said, he also answered some questions in Yup'ik. Then he stepped away from my side, closer to the front of the group, turned and faced me. Then he asked me in English, "So it is like a petition?"

Briefing on regulation proposals was to brief. "No, every proposal has to be considered by the Board. Then" Ralph signaled for a pause, stepped back to my side, turned and faced the group and translated what I had said.

He then stepped back out in front of me and said "Go on."

He's going to get tired walking back and forth. Guess it helps keep which language to use clear. I bet translating is hard. Where was I, everything has to be considered. "But proposals that have been reviewed and accepted by the advisory committee and others are better, but they still might not pass."

Ralph translated, an elderly man stepped forward and spoke in Yup'ik. Ralph stepped away from me, turned to face me and asked "Who is this advisory committee?"

Who is the advisory committee, don't have any idea who they are. What should I say? Honesty works best. "I don't know who they are? I thought you would know? Mr. Geiger said every village has a member." Ralph stepped back to my side while signaling for a pause. Before pausing I finished my thought "Isn't there an advisory committee member here?"

Ralph translated for quite a while. *Did I say that much? Good, Ralph just said "Doy", maybe this is almost over. I'm sweating like a pig.* **Pigs don't sweat.** *Yeah, that helps.*

Everyone's talking in Yup'ik now. The Virgins are sitting over there on that wagon. Should I go sit with them. Segregation? Ralph seems to be calling for quiet. Most everyone is turning towards someone there in the middle. An advisory board member? The old man had the floor and spoke softly in Yup'ik. Clearly, he couldn't be heard very far away because people were turning, whispering to people behind them. When the noise became too much he would stop until the ripple of whispers worked its way to the outer edge. Then he would start again. *This is taking forever. Wonder what he's saying?* Finally, it was over.

Ralph turned back to me and said "They don't listen to the advisory committee. The proposal is probably a waste of time but I will fill one out, circulate it for as much support as we can get. He says a proposal won't open the fishery for more fish until next year. How do we get it opened now? Ralph sounded like he was getting a little angry. He stepped back to my side, fuming if I read him right.

"I don't know how much the Board listens to the advisory committee. I have never been involved in making regulations." Ralph was signaling for a break. Ralph translated.

I added "I can ask on radio how to get it reopened." Another translation. Then Ralph stepped away from me, turned and faced me again. A lot of discussion in angry and demanding tones in the background. "You go get on the radio and come back with an answer?"

What happened to Yup'ik politeness? Should I tell them I'm going to the radio and hide until after radio schedule? Naw, probably burn the office. "No one will be listening until our scheduled reporting time at five this afternoon. *Give me half an hour to get ready for CB.* I will ask how you can have the fishery reopened then and report the results on a special fishery update at five thrity. OK?"

Ralph stomped up to my side and translated to an increasingly restless crowd that clearly understood most of what I had said and wasn't happy about it. Then he marched back out in between the crowd and me. Turned facing me and said "What do you do if you have an emergency?"

What do we do, if there is an emergency? First aid training and kit. Get on the CB and call for help like everyone else. Is this an emergency? None of those answers work or will satisfy.

The boat sinking was kind of an emergency? "When my boat sank, everyone knows about that," I was interrupted by laughter, most knew the story. Some people seemed to be explaining the story to an unknowing neighbor.

"I had to wait until someone found me. Then reported losing the boat on the radio schedule.

Guess like everyone else I have to wait for help from the people here."

Ralph looked a little frustrated but the crowd had gotten a good laugh at my expense so seemed less hostile. *Humor is a good thing to use, especially if it's about you. Don't remember that from Speech. <u>Maybe tell professor. She's a little older but cute. I'm not her student</u> <u>anymore</u>,* **Be real.** *Wait until you see if your still alive in five minutes.*

"You can't talk to Geiger before five?" Ralph confirmed.

"No, I'm sorry." To my surprise Ralph walked up beside me and gave a short translation then returned to his spot between me and the crowd. *Nice of him to be serving this dual role.*

Ralph returned to his position as spokesman. "You tell Geiger to open again on Thursday when you talk to him."

Was that a question or a statement? "No, we work for Mr. Geiger, he's our boss. I will tell him about the meeting and what you want. But I don't tell him what to do."

Ralph turned to the group, there was a huddle, as much as a group of a couple hundred can huddle. There was a long discussion.

Then Ralph turned to me "This man has something to say." The group turned facing an elder, a perfect picture, *Where's my camera. H*is clothing was all traditional gear, a summer parki squirrel[35] parka, seal skin waterproof boots, his face was weathered, he was a very small man. He spoke in Yup'ik for what seemed to me a long time. Fishgame was said a few times but his voice was steady with no emotion. Although his words seemed to be making the crowd very serious. "Doy", he stepped back to lean against a piece of old machinery where he had been.

---

[35] Parki squirrels are large ground squirrels found in the mountains above tree line. Their lighter fur is used to make summer parkas.

Ralph didn't look happy when he turned to face me. "He said back when the commercial fishery first opened there wasn't enough fish to eat and people starved. After fishgame took over there were always enough fish for winter."

Good to know. "Is that all?" *Should I point out how long he spoke?*

"Yes." There was a murmur through the group. Ralph looked back "You tell Geiger what happened and what we demand!" People were drifting away from the edges of the group.

"Yes, I will. Are there any other questions?" *Why say that. Been here long enough.*

"No, you can go."

Didn't know I couldn't leave? "OK, thank you everyone for coming," and I said to departing backs. "Ralph, thanks for translating." "Goodbye" he said over his shoulder.

❦

"Geiger isn't here. Won't be back until Monday. What do you need?"

In three short sentences, I told Fritz about the meeting and demand to know how to reopen the fishery. He asked me to wait until the end of radio schedule.

"Bethel back to Emmonak."

"Emmonak Fish and Game back to Bethel."

"Hang on while I give Carl[36] a call at home."

"Fish and Game Emmonak standing by."

Probably lose my job for stirring up all this trouble. Where did Geiger go until Monday?

Hope Mr. Yanagowa doesn't get pissed about Fritz disturbing him? Fritz is a good guy. Handles all kinds of shit the field camps come up with. Guess we're a field camp? Most don't get a solid roof with a store and cafeteria next door.

"Fish and Game Emmonak this is Fish and Game Bethel."

"Fish and Game Emmonak back."

"Carl says Tech Threes don't do public meetings. King fishery is closed. Have to wait for chum season."

"Fish and Game Emmonak. Thanks."

---

[36] Carl Yanagowa was the Kuskokwim Area biologist.

"Fish and Game Bethel out."

"Thank you Fritz, err Bethel. Fish and Game Emmonak out."

"Sounds like maybe you shouldn't have done the meeting?" Gary gave voice to my dark thoughts.

"Yeah, there goes my career. Assuming I don't get lynched after the fishery update." I said.

"Think they'll lynch both of us? Or maybe just nail the door shut and set the place on fire while we sleep." Gary said cheerfully.

"Do you want first watch?" I asked in the same teasing tone.

"Nah, we just need to take it easy. There will be a lot of grumbling but like you told me these are good people. They won't do anything crazy. I'm sure Geiger will understand why we did the meeting. Hell, he might even appreciate you saving him a trip." Gary said.

❦

The fishery update seemed to go on forever that night. How many ways can you answer the same question "When will fishing reopen?" Sometimes there were interesting commentaries. Like "It's closed, bears eat salmon we no catch. Fishgame sells bear licenses big money. Don't care about Yup'iks. Chums only good for dogs, sick people." Even a golden oldie, according to Geiger, "fish thick in river, you can walk across on backs." After every question and commentary, I would transmit that the fishery was closed until chum salmon season. Gary took over when my mouth gave out. I poured the last thick cup of rewarmed coffee, *What's wrong with me. Hero complex. Gary doesn't mind helping.* The pauses between callers became longer and we continued taking turns. We finally decided it was time to sign off when the chatter settled into Yup'ik only.

"Whew, that was a long session. Interesting, back on campus that level of discussion would have degenerated into swearing and other verbal abuse." Gary commented.

"Yeah, even the public meeting today stayed civil. Guess it's part of the culture. Small village, trapped together all winter and no escape. If you don't get along, you don't fit in." I theorized.

"Stick to biology." Gary told me.

Next morning the office door burst open with such violence that Gary and I both jumped to our feet expecting what we didn't know.

"Where is that damn alibi Mike?" roared a big Kass'ak in bright yellow raingear from hat to floor. His raingear was still wet, his muddy boots leaving tracks on the floor. His presence seemed to take up all the space in the room.

"He's in Bethel." We answered in unison.

"He closed the fucking fishery here and he's in Bethel! Who or what are you fuckers?"

I noticed for the first time a much smaller embarrassed looking Yup'ik man about our ages standing in the hallway watching the tirade.

"We're fish tech threes. I'm Gary Foster and he's Kim Francisco. Who do we have the pleasure of meeting? Would you like a coffee?"

"Your fucking parasites on the state. How can fucking Alibi Mike close the fishery when he's not even here. Do you want coffee?" He finished, turning to the younger man.

"Yes" came the barely audible reply. Gary stepped around the dripping man into the kitchen leaving me as the parasite in focus.

"I'm Arnold Akers. How can you be monitoring the fishery when you don't know who I am? You've never been to our plant. You sit here all-day drinking coffee!"

Akers, that handful of fish tickets that Geiger takes care of. Probably shouldn't tell the fucker that, looks like he's ready for a fist fight. "Yes sir. Your fish tickets are added into the catch totals. The king salmon harvest guideline has been exceeded so the fishery has closed." I said.

"You mean the fucking quota, don't use your bureaucratic weasel words with me. Of course, it's been taken. We're having the best fucking king run ever! Albi Mike's in Bethel celebrating putting me out of business and doesn't even know what's happening out here. You two parasites are sitting here warm and clean. Never even been outside or put a net in the water. Probably don't even know the difference between a king and a chum. Their just numbers on yellow scraps of paper. Does anyone even check on what you are doing or if you can add two and two? Damn Albi Mike just sits on his butt in Bethel and listens to you parasites buzzing on the radio. Then the great man gets to close off our lifeline. How does he expect me to support my village out there in the willows?"

Akers seemed to have actually paused for an answer. Gary spoke from behind, where he had been having coffee with the younger man, "His Supervisor Mr. Regnart was out here checking.

"Regnart! That boney assed college kid. He couldn't find his ass with both hands if it were on fire! Don't tell me about Regnart. I know all about him. He was screwing us for years before Alibi Mike came. Regnart, Regnart, God help us if Regnart's in charge. Thought I ran him out. You know I came out of those willows twenty years ago and I can go right back in again." He was stabbing my breast bone hard with his index finger. "Bill Egan[37] landed at the end of my dock when he was campaigning. Thought because we had been in the army together

I'd let him give his speech." His finger was still pounding on my chest. "I went out to the end of the dock. When he opened the plane door I looked in and said "Bill did you bring your own grub?" "No" says he so I told him you can't get out here. Leave now and he did."

So, go back into your precious willows you fucking jerk. Just quite spitting in my face.

Can't say that. *Remember what they talked about when they were here.*

"I overheard Mr. Regnart tell Mr. Geiger that he would let Steve Penoyer…"

"**That beady eyed politician Penoyer!![38]**! I, aw, his, He can't tell a fucking sockeye from a Coho." He tore his rainhat off slapping it repeatedly on his thigh. His face turned purple. He turned and stormed out the still open door.

Gary followed the younger man to the door, closing it gently. Then he returned to where I was still anchored to the floor. "Well, you always know the right thing to say. Got him out of here. Wow, what a force of nature." Gary said.

"Yeah, after I mentioned Penoyer I thought I was going to have use CPR on the fucker. Don't think I could've given him the kiss of life though. Bleah." I said as the possible moral dilemma froze my brain. "Wonder if he'll be back? His son, Billy, seemed like a nice guy." Gary concluded.

During my next twenty-two years with the Department seemed like every closure from abalone to salmon produced the same complaints.

---

[37] Former Governor of Alaska

[38] Division Director

Commercial fishing is one of the few occupations where a neutral nonparticipant tells the worker when and how much they can work.

It's rarely taken well.

FISH TICKETS

Dobson skillfully landed the float equipped Supercub on the Yukon River opposite the village of Saint Mary. "Kim, wind and current are bad for beaching. You get out on the float and grab the bowline, soon as the prop stops, jump ashore and pull us in." Crackled my instructions threw the head set.

I struggled against the prop wash pushing the Cub's split door open. Fastening the top half to the upper fuselage and the bottom half to the lower. Even at a taxi against this wind the propwash was strong. I stepped out onto the float, the full force of the prop wash now hitting me. With my left hand gripping the hand grip over the engine. I squatted down, leaning out over the float. Then seized the yellow bowline out of the river where it lay alongside the float. Standing with my prize, I looked over at Dobson. He nodded and hit the throttle, the propwash and flying spray forcing me to duck my head into the cabin. Watching the approaching shore through the windscreen and the spinning propeller I prepared to jump.

The plane's floats scrapped bottom, the engine stopped, the prop stopped, I raced forward on the float, leaping for the shore. My lead foot hit something soft and slippery when I landed, instead of hard gravel, it flew out from under me. As I tried to recover my following left foot landed on an equally soft slippery surface and I did a face plant into the soft slime. My nose identified rotten fish, the jerk and pull in my hand told me the plane was trying to escape. ***Plane is first priority.*** *Screw the plane, we're in a pile of dead fish.* I rolled onto my back, freeing my left hand so I had both hands on the rope. Dobson was almost helpless with laughter as he climbed out of the Cub's door onto the float. I sat-up in the slime and sludge of the rotten fish. Using the bowline as an anchor I pulled myself to my feet. Dobson still laughing, made it to the bowline on the left float, tossing it to me. I shuffled through the rotten fish to solid footing, then gently, to protect the floats, pulled the Cub firmly on land, just downstream of the pile of fish.

Dobson stepped off, dry footed.

"PU! Stay upwind. You smell awful." Laughter interrupted Dobson's comments, that I did my best to ignore. Walking upstream of the rotten fish I wadded out as far as my hip boots allowed, then began rinsing off the rotten fish with handfuls of water. "Got 'a give you credit most people would have let go of the plane. Nice job." More laughter. *Glad someone is enjoying this.*

"Yeah be sure and tell Geiger so he can put it on my evaluation." I snarled. *Hey, it is funny. Whimp! It's humiliating.* Cleaned-up as best as I could manage in the cold Yukon water, *at least the big pieces are off,* I trudged ashore. Laid my coat out to dry on the beach and recovered the briefcase from the plane. "I'll be right back. Have to get the fish tickets from the office up there."

Dobson said "I'll wait here with the plane. See if you can find your sense of humor up there."

I climbed the bank to the fish buyer's station and collected the all-important fish tickets. Found out the plane that came to pick up their fish had been too small to take them all. It hadn't come back in time to save the rest so they had dumped them on the beach. I warned them to take them out into the river next time as required by the Department of Environmental Protection. *Being a good little bureaucrat. Hey you were humiliated. Admit it, felt good to have something on them. A bad day can spoil this most mellow official.*

The last laugh was on Dobson. As we were returning to Emmonak he found just having the window open and blasting on me wasn't enough to keep the smell away. He had to fly the Cub in a crabbed attitude, sideways, an uncomfortable way to fly. The open window was almost the windshield in this attitude, which increased the airflow over me. *Just hope some of the smell rubbed off on my seat and stays awhile.*

Fish tickets, receipts the Department gave to the commercial fish buyers, free of charge, aren't very exciting. Collecting them, has its moments. The Commercial Fisheries Division collected the Department's copy which allowed determining the size of the commercial catch, which for adult salmon was their largest mortality. My primary reason for being in Emmonak those first two summers was the collection, tallying, and reporting the totals to the manager. Excited yet?

In my near-death experience, when an old wooden skiff sank, the reason I was in the skiff was collecting fish tickets. Once collected we or I depending on how many employees were available, tallied the number of fish by species and then tallied the number of fishers. Known as fishermen until Governor Sheffield's administration when we went gender neutral and they became fishers.

My second summer I was transferred upriver from Emmonak to Fairbanks to replace the fish ticket editor who had returned to college. I had graduated the previous spring and was looking for a permeant biologist job. I was going through the latest batch of fish tickets, automatically still comparing the name on the license at the top with the signature at the bottom.

Whoa, double check, nope no question they don't match. That's never happened before. I picked-up the ticket and carried it from my desk into Fred Anderson, Assistant Yukon Area biologist. Fred was on the phone but soon finished. "Hi, sorry to disturb you but needed to know if you wanted me to call FWP about this ticket or if you want to call?"

"What's the problem?"

"The fisherman didn't sign it. Someone else did. Looks like someone is loaning or renting their license."

"Show me." I handed him the ticket. Looking his face suddenly drooped. "O God, why him?"

"Is it a friend?" I asked.

"No, it's the Chair of the State Senate budget committee. Shit, I better call protection and see what they want to do? You best forget you saw it."

"Ung, OK, I better get a copy so I can finish the tickets."

Fred hesitated, holding the ticket. "Yeah, get a copy then bring it back. Remember these are confidential."

"Roger." I took the fish ticket from him and copied it. He was on the phone with protection when I returned it, putting it down in front of him. I returned to my desk.

I thought that was the end of it. Fish& Wildlife Protection handled things from there. Luckily for me they kept me anonymous. The grapevine reported that the Senator was very angry and wanted the head of whoever reported him. Once again I feared for my career. Fish tickets do have their exciting moments.

I was fortunate my first two summers in Emmo because there was a huge technological advance in processing fish tickets, an electric adding machine. Hard to imagine what it was like when fish ticket editors used the old "one armed bandit" hand crank adding machine we found in the attic unpacking that first summer. Eleven plus years later a Yukon assistant area biologist wrote the first program for a personal computer to process fish tickets. This advance let us do away with the dreaded dot sheet. A ruled pad of paper with the fishermen's names down the side and the date of each fishing period across the top. Each fish ticket was checked and if it was the first ticket for that fisher a dot was put opposite the name and under the date. If the fisher delivered more than once or to more than one processor no further dots were added. After completing the fish tickets for a fishing period, you counted up the number of dots for that period. Presto! You knew how many fishers had fished. Sounds easy until you start trying to count hundreds of dots.

Multiplying the number of fishers' times, the number of hours in the fishing period gave you fisher-hours. Divide the catch by fisher-hours and you have a standardized catch per fisher-hour, which allows comparison of fish abundance between periods and years. Exciting stuff, time to tune in "NATURE", they mostly skip the science in wildlife management.

Fish tickets did cause some earlier apprehension in Fairbanks that second summer before I arrived. The Fairbanks Fish ticket editor and an assistant had gone to Nenana to pick-up the tickets and sample the fish at a processor there. Mr. Lord, who did think he was the Lord of Nenana, also was a fish buyer and processor. He was angry with the Department over his fine for catching more beavers than allowed the previous winter. Instead of just denying the sampling crew access. His right. He ran them off with a running chainsaw. This resulted in Fred getting a restraining order requiring Mr. Lord to allow the staff to work. I inherited this situation when I transferred into the fish ticket editor job.

"Kim, sorry I can't go to Nenana with you today to introduce you. The subsistence crew didn't have any trouble with Edmund so you shouldn't."

Gulp. *How do you disarm a guy with a chainsaw!* "Ok. My finance has the day off. She asked if she could go along and see the fall colors. She helped with sampling when she visited Emmo last summer. Does a good job on the AWL forms."

"Yeah, take her along. More witnesses the better."

Great! Wittiness. O well she wanted to go. I called the apartment and told her I would be picking her up in ten minutes. The drive down the twisting curving Nenana Highway has scenic overlooks of the Tanana Valley. Marsha and I enjoyed the trip. Following Fred's directions, I found Edmund's with no problem. His was a unique operation rather than just selling his chums to out-of-state buyers he cut, dried, and cold smoked them in the traditional way. He sold the final product to dog mushers, including the National Park Service, for dog food.

As I stepped out of the familiar orange pickup I saw a middle aged, powerfully built man look-up from the table where he was cutting fish with an unwelcoming glare. He came around the table with the knife dripping in his hand. *Do I remind him of the restraining order?*

"Marsha." I turned to tell her to stay in the truck too late. She was already out. Edmund's demeanor changed immediately. He threw the knife back onto the table and with a big smile walked towards us.

Never under estimate the power of beautiful women! "Hi. I'm the new catch sampler and fish ticket editor. Kim Francisco Sir." My outstretched hand hung in empty air.

"Marsha's new too." I don't think Ed had even looked at me, his eyes were locked on Marsha.

"Hi I'm Marsha, Kim's fiancé." She introduced herself.

"Sir can we sample the fish you're working on?" I asked.

"Yeah, yeah." He waved me off like a fly. "Have you ever seen a fish operation before,

Marsha?"

Fluttering her brown eyes and turning on all her charm she answered "No. They were done drying salmon when I visited Emmonak."

"Let me show you around." With a protective arm behind her back he lead her off to show her his fish wheel where the process started.

A little concerned I started to follow. Marsha turned saying "I'll be all right. You just sample. Unless you need me?"

She didn't sound or look like she cared to be rescued. "No. I can handle it you guys go ahead." *Hope I read her signals right.*

I sampled fish while they walked around the operation. I did see her decline a boat ride to see the river. Ed looked disappointed but the tour continued. I finished the uncleaned fish but was short of the goal of 120. Fred had anticipated that in his instructions so I finished the sample with just scales plucked from the drying fish. Marsha and Ed returned just as I was finishing.

"I do need to pick-up the fish tickets then we can get out of your hair, Sir." I said to Mr. Lord.

Ed said "No trouble." And stepped into the office shack for the tickets.

I asked Marsha "Everything go alright?"

"Yes. He's very sweet. Don't know what you guys are afraid of."

Fish tickets in hand we headed back to Fairbanks. Marsha told me all about Ed's operation. He also taught her how to make fish head soup. Which he said was vital to the success of a marriage. Fortunately, Marsha never saw a need to prepare it for me.

Fish tickets are dull, repetitive and extremely valuable, I once explained the system to a visiting fisheries manager from Peru, she was amazed. She left with a book of fish tickets, hoping she could add such a system in Peru. Perhaps I should say fish tickets were, I understand processors hand in a thumb drive with all the data or send the catch figures in over the web now.

DEPUTY PROTECTION OFFICER

We couldn't find enough kings on Monday to fill the sampling goal! "Shit all the tenders are in. So, no more kings. Maybe we should go up to the Coop and see if their still unloading fish."

"Kim, don't get your panties in a bunch. I'm sure this happens every year. The king run is coming to an end. Geiger won't mind. You're not competing with anyone. We've put in over 12 hours today. Time to eat and sleep. Tomorrow is the Fourth. We get a day off." Gary lectured.

"Fuck it. Your right let's call it a day. We did try hard."

As we walked back to the office a Fish& Wildlife Protection Supercub on floats taxied in off the river and up the muddy ramp leading to the boat yard.

"Looks like Dobson." Gary said.

"Yeah, isn't that a great airplane."

"You are a real flying nut."

"I sure am. Wonder if I should go into Protection instead of biology so I can fly."

Dobson, a man about my size, just shy of six feet and heavy set, in the tan Fish and Wildlife Protection Officer uniform climbed out. He took a duffle bag and riot gun[39] out of the plane. He walked over to join us at the office door. "Hi do you mind a guest?"

"Welcome back. Want me to take that?" I reached for the duffle bag handle.

"Yeah. Thanks", He dropped the duffle into my outstretched hand.

"Did you patrol the opening?"

"Yes, you have a good bunch of fishermen here. Didn't find any early starters and everyone I checked was legal. Gave a couple warnings about buoys. No body fishing late." Dobson summarized his day.

As I led the way to the bunk room I asked "What's that about buoys?"

---

[39] A short barreled, twelve-gauge pump action Remington 870 shotgun.

"People have beach combed sea lion buoys[40] that the crabbers lost. They put them on their gear without changing the vessel number to their own. A technical violation. I warned them but didn't ticket anyone." He explained.

Sitting down next to the radio, I picked up my clip board and started writing.

"I didn't think I said anything noteworthy." Dobson said.

"Always looking for things to add to the fishery report. It gets a hum drum otherwise." I answered.

"He aspires to be another Wolfman Jack. Wolfman Kim." Added Gary

"How does an aspiring DJ end up working for Com Fish in Emmonak?"

"Gary exaggerates. I'm a Wildlife Management Major at the U of A and aspire to work for ADF&G. Gary is the misfit. He aspires to be an attorney." I shot back.

"What brought you to Emmonak?" Dobson asked Gary.

"The money. Tough going to college and supporting a student wife, Fish and Game paid better than interning in a law office. Which is what she's doing."

"A double threat! The money will come. We got a report a bootlegger was bringing in a load of hooch for tomorrow's fourth celebration. You guys heard anything about it?" Dobson asked.

"No. That's odd would've thought someone in the mukai would have mentioned it." I said.

"Mukai?"

"He means the sauna, he's going native." Gary added.

"You guys have a sauna!" Dobson said with anticipation.

"The village does. Just opened. It's part of the new drinking water plant. Includes men and women's showers and a laundromat." Gary finished.

"Sounds nice. Do either of you have a needle and thread?" Dobson asked.

"Yeah, I'm an Eagle scout, always prepared. I'll get it." *One of my few accomplishments.*

Nice to get in a brag. I walked into the bedroom and grabbed my sewing kit.

---

[40] The crabbers in the Bering Sea and Gulf of Alaska had to switch to a very large and very tough buoy for their pots to increase their visibility and sea lions found them fun to play with. Smaller buoys were quickly destroyed by the rough play.

"Hope you like ham." Gary said from the kitchen.

"Ham is better than I expected. Beggars can't be choosers. How did you guys rate ham?" Dobson asked.

"Rate? They brought cases of the stuff. Guess the budget was cut so there're making quantity purchases of grub. Don't know if it was personal taste or availability but instead of beef stew or chili, we got twenty or so canned hams and a couple of cases of canned bacon and SPAM. Good thing no one is Jewish around here." Gary filled in as he twisted the key opening the can.

"Even I might get tired of that much ham. Dobson answered.

"We also have half a case of Spaghettios left over from last year. For variety." I added.

"How much longer are you here for?" Dobson asked.

"Kim's probably here for the duration, early September. I'm supposed to have just a week left. A week too long." Gary answered from the kitchen.

"Don't you love me anymore?" I asked in a hurt voice.

"NO. I want my wife." Gary returned.

"Now, now boys." Dobson said. "Do you think this color thread is a close enough match to my pants?" Dobson held a light brown spool of thread from my sewing kit against his pant leg.

"Hmm, going to be noticeable, where's the tear? I asked.

"Here." Dobson spread his legs, revealing a split seam in his crotch.

"People don't usually look at the crotch too much. Hard to see anyway. Probably will work.

Current style is if it doesn't match make it really not match. Maybe the red or black?" I suggested helpfully.

"Hey, we get evaluated on deportment. I'll go with the brown. It will work till I can get home to my wife." He threaded a needle, broke off enough thread to moor the Queen Mary and spread his legs wide and began trying to sew the torn seam. I grabbed my camera and took a couple of quick shots before laughter got the better of me and Gary.

"What's so funny, what the hell you doing with the camera?" Dobson asked angrily looking up from his work.

"He had to record this fiasco. Where did you learn to sew?" Asked Gary,

Dobson had a brown tangle of thread that looked like he was trying to weave a patch of new brown fabric across his tighty whities.

"You clowns can do better?"

"I'm cooking supper." Answered Gary.

"Yes, I can do better. Even have a merit badge to prove it, back home." In case he asked to see it.

Dobson was looking into his crotch dubiously. He was justifiably concerned over allowing a stranger to work with a needle and thread in such a sensitive area.

Laughing I said "You'll have to take your pants off for two reasons. First, you have to get the tension off the seam to sew them properly. Second, I wouldn't go in there on a bet."

"Yeah, but I don't have an extra pair."

"We won't see anything we haven't seen already." Gary chimed in from the kitchen.

"I think we have a blanket you can put over your legs. In case anyone comes in to protect your modesty" I choked out, still amused. "Or you could try a pair of mine, will 36's fit?

"Nope, have to be the blanket. It's not real warm in here."

"OK" I went into the bedroom and retrieved one of the military surplus blankets that had been laying on a vacant top bunk ever since they turned up when we were bringing the mattresses down out of the attic. Returning with the blanket, I handed it to Dobson, who was standing, bare legged, holding his pants. "Here you can keep your legs warm." "Kinda of dusty." He said spreading the blanket and a cloud of dust.

Taking his pants, I said "Gary, we have to shake the blankets after we sweep." "Haw!" He replied.

I sat down with the pants "What a mess." I pulled the spider's web of brown thread out of his pants. Broke off a reasonable length of thread, tied a new jam knot, and turned the pants inside out. I pulled the seam together and stitched it up. "There almost as good as new." I handed Dobson his pants back," Now whatever you do don't spread your legs or squat until your wife can put in a patch. Or you buy a larger pair of pants."

Gary announced supper. Ham with a canned pineapple-brown sugar glaze, canned corn, and pilot bread. He had a cake in the oven for desert.

"Wow, Gary, thank you, you really put yourself out for our guest." Dobson said.

"Not really, you just picked the right night." Then the tales, short and tall began.

After a pleasant morning of sharing breakfast, more stories, reading and Dobson catching up on paper work. We were working our way through a fried SPAM sandwich lunch, when frantic knocking started at the door.

"That's strange, people don't usually knock." I said going to the door.

An elder, unknown to me was standing there "Need help. Trouble. Big trouble. Over there." He said pointing in the direction of the NC "helipad", really just a spot they kept clear for the Bell 47 helicopter, just like in MASH. The fisheries' manager son, who was also the owner/pilot, had brought it up thinking it would help manage the tenders.

"OK. I'll come. I have to put my boots on." I said.

"Not you. One with gun." The elder explained he was after Dobson. This was big trouble.

Stepping back inside I said to Dobson "There seems to be a problem requiring a law enforcement officer."

Dobson was on his feet and moving towards the door. "Either of you deputized?" "Not me." Answered Gary.

"I am." I answered with a mixture of concern and excitement.

"Grab my shotgun, you're my back-up."

He was out the door and talking to the elder. I jammed on my rubber boots and picked-up the riot gun from the top bunk where it had lain safely all night and followed. Not being the owner/user of a pump action shotgun, I was following, trying to catch up, familiarize myself with the shotgun, trying not to fall on my face as I took glances to see what this was all about. We arrived at the helicopter where Tommy Jr. was drunkenly waving and axe and screaming something about Kass'aks, NC and others who were keeping the Yup'ik people down. Then with a resounding CRACK! He buried the axe into the helicopter's plastic bubble. The pilot/owner burst out of the gathered crowd, slamming Tommy onto the ground. The axe went flying. He jumped on Tommy's chest, grabbing him by the shoulders, pounding his head onto the ground.

Pulling handcuffs from his belt Dobson gave me my instructions "Just stand there showing the gun, if someone tries to stop me just rack a round into the chamber. That's usually plenty." Then he was gone and behind the pilot who was raising Tommy for another smash into the ground. Too fast to follow a cuff appeared on one wrist, both arms were pulled from Tommy and both wrists were handcuffed behind the pilot's back. Dobson stood-up bringing the pilot to his feet and off Tommy. I started forward, thinking I'd check Tommy for injuries.

"Stand there!" Dobson ordered as he quick marched a protesting pilot back towards the NC office. The famous murmur went through the gathered crowd of villagers. Tommy lay on the ground by himself. Then shaking his head, he managed to sit-up with some difficulty. A few minutes passed and he struggled to his feet. Then Dobson came out of the NC fisheries office and headed our way. Tommy saw him and took off threw the crowd.

"STOP!" commanded Dobson, but Tommy was gone.

Now you'll be in trouble. Let the prisoner escape. *Was he my prisoner? Dobson told me to stand here. I couldn't shoot safely into so many people. I wouldn't shoot, Tommy, he might be my brother-in-law. Shit.*

"You did good, Kim. Take the shotgun back to the office. I'll finish up here." Dobson told me.

"I did? Thanks, but what about Tommy?" "You knew that kid?" Dobson asked.

"Yeah, he's my girlfriend's brother." *Is Irene really your girlfriend? You've only held hands.*

Opening his notebook Dobson quickly wrote Tommy's name down. "How old is he?"

"He's sixteen."

"OK. I'm going to go see if my prisoner has calmed down. See you at the office when this is finished up."

"Right." As I turned to leave I heard a large outboard racing on the river. Turning to look, it was Tommy in his boat headed upstream past the village as fast as his boat would go.

⚜

"Welcome back. The shotgun is back on that top bunk. You want coffee?" I asked Dobson latter when he returned.

"Yeah, just what I need another coffee." Dobson said.

Sarcastically? I choose to take it for a yes and picked up our cups; got Dobson a fresh cup and a warm-up for me.

"Well what'd I miss?" Asked Gary, looking up from his book.

Dobson explained "I told them there isn't much of a juvenile justice system out here so not a lot we could do to the kid. If they didn't insist on an arrest for property damage, I'd let the pilot go without charging him for assault and battery. They thought giving up a misdemeanor for a felony was a good deal. So, it's all over. Guess I'll pack up and head into Bethel."

Sadly, Tommy was found dead, smashed into the bow of his boat by the outboard motor the next morning. He had hit the river bank so fast that the engine broke the transom then carried Tommy into the bow. Irene took his death very hard. She wouldn't see me afterwards.

THE SAUNA

A big change in village life happened with the opening of the new water-plant/laundromat/shower building. Opening day, the line was too long. But the next day the commercial fishery was open. Gary and I loaded our packs with dirty clothes walked down to the deserted new facility. We loaded a couple of washers. Then seriously discussed taking the dirty clothes off our backs and streaking to the showers. Good sense caused us to settle for flipping a coin.

"Heads, damn it you won you fucker. I should know better, I always lose."

"Now, now Kim. Most of your clothes are going to be clean." Gary said as he stripped in the changing room, handed me his clothes and stepped into the men's shower area. I took his clothes out to his washer and stuffed them in.

Why do I let people talk me into flipping coins? I always lose, damn it. There's no one around, should just streaked out of the laundromat to the showers. What a damn coward.

People are streaking everywhere.

I stepped out of the changing room into the shower stalls where a narrow hallway, with a wooden lattice work on top of the linoleum, lead past five or six shower stalls to a cedar door.

Wow, a sauna! This is going to be great. Better make a stop for a quick shower before I take my filthy body into the sauna.

Stepping inside I found Gary already on the top bench.

"This is going to make Emmo the garden camp of Alaska." I greeted him as I climbed up the two rows of benches to the top one. Gary had the prime seat against the interior wall, overlooking the tray of hot lava rocks on top of an oil burning heater. The thermometer over my head read 110 degrees.

"It's still a little cool. I cranked the thermostat up as high as it will go. We should get 120 pretty soon." Gary told me. We both sat back for a relaxing sweat.

This is odd. Back home when it gets this hot we seek out cool basements or air-conditioned buildings. Panel it in cedar and you seek it out for relaxation. If aliens ever do arrive it's going to be hard to explain some of our actions.

The door opened and three village elders came in with the cool blast. One carried a sauce pan filled with water. A plastic cup floated in the water. All three had tight bunches of grass about six inches long, two inches wide and an inch thick. The grass was tied together by pieces of old terry cloth, like they tore strips off an old wash cloth. The three sat down on the second lowest bench below Gary and me. The one with the water pan was closest to the heater.

"Hi" "Camai" we greeted the men.

They just nodded their heads as they settled in. There was a brief exchange in Yup'ik, the one with the pan threw a cup of water onto the rocks. A small cloud of steam rose, but most of the water settled into the rock pan and began sizzling. Warmer air circulated through my hair.

When the sizzling stopped, the waterman hit the rocks with another splash of water. The thermometer was now past 120, the end of the scale. Very little water made it into the pan, all of it turning to steam when it hit the rocks. Hot steamy air washed over my face and upper body.

Our three companions smiled with satisfaction and exchanged a few words in Yup'ik. Now the waterman really set to his task. Occasionally, he would use too much water, the water-cooled rocks wouldn't turn it to steam. It sizzled into steam on the bottom of the pan. My skin was beginning to burn. Gary headed for the door, his place taken by the waterman.

This is a dare. I can take it if these old guys can take it. That cool blast when Gary left sure felt good. Waterman is doing his best to get rid of the fresh air and me. Skin on my legs is too hot. **Go down, second bench.**

This made room for all three on the upper bench. They dipped the grass bundles into water. Then began breathing through the wet bundles. *That's not fair.* **Down to first row. Lungs can't take this heat.** *Geez buddy give the water a rest. He's trying to burn me out. If he can take it so can I damn it.* The thermometer was past the maximum temp of 130. **First bench**. I dropped to the first bench. The oil burner in the heater turned off. A discussion in Yupik between breaths on the wet grass. *Must be a safety thermostat.* The elder closest to the thermometer reached up and pushed the indicator needle back to 100. The burner reignited. My nemesis resumed making steam. *I can't take it. Already lost. Forced to lowest bench.*

I burst out through the door into the cool air. I stepped into the first cold stainless-steel shower stall. To dizzy to stand, I sank to the bottom and took a seat. After a couple of minutes, I stood and took my first cold then hot shower in two months. *Damn that feels good.* After finishing the greatest shower of my life, I was toweling off near the sauna door. *What are those old guys chanting in there.*

The door opened just enough for one of the elders to slip out. He picked up a bar of soap and a wash cloth off the bench and slipped back in.

What's that about? He's red as a lobster. An interesting dare. Next time, something to cool the hot air. I'm as tough as they are. You win today. Was it worth it. What are they doing now? Another mystery. Not peeking in to see what it's all about. Nothing like being squeaky clean. Back to the office.

Gary was waiting for me in the laundromat. Our clothes in a dryer. "How long did you last?"

"Not a lot longer than you. Thought I was going to pass out when I escaped. Guess they proved their point. I'll be ready next time."

"How you going to be ready?" Gary wondered aloud.

"A wet wash rag to breath threw. Their secret was those bundles of wet grass. They started breathing threw those after you ran out. I'm as tough as they are." I said.

"Hey don't take it so personally. It's just a sauna. Hey, this place was quite the feat in prefabrication. Where do they clean the water?" Gary asked knowing I had spent some time talking to Mr. Redfox the manager.

"In the back, out of sight, there's a section where water from a well is treated and made potable." I explained. "It's really river water. In limnology, we had learned that in addition to the visible surface water, rivers flow through the soil to the sides and below the bottom, depending on the porosity of the river bed. In permafrost, like here, the warmer river water thaws the surrounding permafrost, as a result wells near the river often have water available. Silt is gone but bacteria still on board." I explained.

"Can't you drill threw the permafrost to clean water?" Gary asked.

"Probably but it would require drilling hundreds, maybe thousands of feet to penetrate the permafrost. Then it would be a toss-up if you found water, oil or gas." I replied.

"Or nothing. Which is probably more likely. " Gary said.

Our conversation lasted through folding and packing our clothes. We headed back to the office. We passed an open shed with an old-style ringer washing machine visible through the open door. Gary noticed it and asked "Is that a washer?"

"Yeah. Like the one I grew-up with. Except ours didn't have that gasoline engine juryrigged to it. Just plugged in. Your Mom didn't have a ringer-washer?"

"Not that I remember." Was Gary's surprising answer.

"There are a few old-style ringer washers in Emmo. Electricity is recent here. Pretty ingenious to hook up a pony engine. The owners add dirty clothes and detergent, a couple of buckets of water and fire that sucker up. Then you have to drain and refill to rinse. Shortly after arriving I saw one thrashing away, it reminded me of my mother's, except noisier." "The electric one had to be quieter?" Gary put in.

"Not much. Mom's beast, was electric but was confined to the basement. My father finally gave up anchoring it and plugged in a long extension cord so it was free to vibrate across the floor. When it hit the wall, it would change course and head off in a new direction until it reached a wall. Use to be great entertainment on hot summer days to sit on the cool basement stairs and watch the Beast dance around the basement." I said.

"It also was fun to feed the wet clothing into the ringer after the rinse cycle. Didn't save Mom much work, she was unwavering in her supervision, to keep our fingers and hands out of the ringer. The warnings had caused me to wonder what would really happen if the ringer "caught" me. My fingers were dangerously close as I tried to get caught. Cost me a lot of slapped hands and loss of my ringer privileges."

"Do you think everything is a personal dare?" Gary asked me.

"Sort of. After seeing a friend's sister's arm, after she returned from the hospital after going through a ringer. I kept my fingers away. Found out why my grandmother called the ringer a "mangler." I replied.

Gary and I became the envy of the other camps. Flat Island was close enough that the test fish crew soon discovered it wasn't too long a trip to Emmonak. They had to check the nets every twelve hours. The lure of clean clothes and body was surprisingly strong. They joined Gary in telling me that my continuing quest to outlast the elders was stupid. But I was ten years old again and kept risking first degree or worst burns to be the last man standing err sitting. The first trick was breathing through something wet. That went a long way. Next, I followed the elders onto my knees on the sweaty floor facing the heater. We would be in a line shoulder to shoulder, butts against the door and wall. Faces to the floor as low as possible where the air was just a little cooler. Many a person opened the door behind us, offering a blessed rush of cool air, only to slam it tight. Not sure which was worst, the blast of heat coming out or the sight of four sweaty asses. After that I joined the chant, hah, hah, hah, as long as you lasted. Not sure why that helped but it did. I soon was able to outlast all but a few real pros. But I hadn't won yet.

❦

Many things changed in July: summer chum fishery ended and Gary left. The test fish crew came back and turned into the subsistence survey crew heading out upriver. I was living with a woman for the first time in my life. But I still hadn't been the last one out the sauna door.

Slipped into my flip-flops as protection against a reoccurrence of athlete's foot and entered the men's shower. I rinsed off and checked in the sauna. Steam clouds came pouring out as I quickly stepped in to save the heat. Three of the elders I had taken a "steam" with in the past welcomed me "Cama-I". Then the one on the top bench patted it with his hand inviting me to join him saying "You have Yup'ik wife, can you stay in mukai like Yup'ik man?" This made everyone laugh. *Laugh now. We'll see who laughs last. Marie isn't my wife. Should I correct him? No today we make sure we don't get burned out.*

A real mukai, is a small tundra sod hut where the men gathered around a large driftwood fire. When they were "done" they crawled out the door where their wives rinsed them off with river water. The sauna had exchanged wives for shower-stalls and driftwood for an oil-fired heater but not much else changed.

The elders had removed the thermostat during the sauna's first week to allow the temperature to rise above 120 degrees. With no control on the

84

temperatures the cedar safety railing around the heater was beginning to char away, from the inside. That and common sense should have told me what a foolish contest I was trying to win. First the water thrower moved down to the second lower bench. Henry[41], the elder next to me, raised his head from his chest enough to glace in my direction. Seeing me still there, he stayed put. The three of them were breathing through wet grass, I was breathing through a wet wash rag rolled into a cylinder. The man with the dipper continued, soon slipping down to the second bench. The man next to him followed. Henry and I were the only ones left on the top bench. Finally, Henry gave up and slid down to join the others who were now on the third and lowest bench.

The thermometer on the wall opposite my head maxed out at 130 degrees. The pointer was past that. "**You're nuts**" Richard said. "*We are winning.*" After what seemed like a long time, my skin was burning. **Point made, move before your hurt!**

I slid down to the second bench. *One Mississippi, two Mississippi, sixty Mississippi,* **long enough.** There was room on the lowest bench now since the dipper-man and his pal were on the floor. I slid down. What a relief, it was hard to believe the temperature could change so much.

Still more water and steam, the temperature on the lowest bench continued to climb. Finally, Henry sank to the floor leaving room for me. O*ne hundred and twenty Mississippi* **Two minutes ENOUGH.** *Proved my point.* What point? I took my place on the floor. The elders began chanting "Hah, hah, hah…" through their grass air coolers. I tried to join in the chant but I couldn't get the rhythm. *Head swimming.* I kept my mouth closed around my washrag that was drying out and heating up. *Their cheating, dipping the grass bundles in the water pan. Slide that pan over here you bastard!* Someone open the door and left. Bless the cool air. *Swirlies starting.*

The dipper, our torturer, crawled to the door. Another cascade of cool air poured over my back as he slipped out. Henry took over the water, quickly throwing water onto the hot stones to restore the heat and pain. *Got to be second degree burns on my back.* **Get Out!** *No don't wimp out.* Henry passed the water to me. I dipped my breathing rag in the pan. *Cool air in lungs. I'm saved.* **Henry plays fair.** Henry resumed the torture.

---

[41] My apologies to my friend but his name has slipped my mind. Made this one up.

Fair play, thank you. Can you get third degree burns in a sauna? If he can take it, you can.

He chanted and threw water. *I'm to dizzy to stand, can you be to dizzy to crawl?* **Chant don't think. That's the secret.** Dragging himself over the threshold Henry finally gave up and escaped out the door.

I reviled in the cool draft and my victory. I didn't throw any water on the rocks to reheat the room. *Count to 120, that will show them.* **Ninety's enough GET OUT.** *Can't find handle. Need to look. Can't raise head. There it is. Cold air never felt so good. First stall empty. Cold steel. Just lay here. You Won!* **What did we win.** *Respect, honor, pride!* **Remember what Falstaff said about those.** *Remember what Bible says about pride. Guess Aretha might be right about respect. How long have I laid here? Think can stand.* I did stand but had to lean against the wall and grab the shower controls to make it. Leaning against the wall I turned the cold water on, it sprayed down my back. I was too close to the wall for it to it my body. *Cold shower never felt so good. Wonder if those three left this closest stall for me on purpose. Nice.*

⁂

Marie lectured me about stupid male pride as she gently dubbed vinegar on my back. Being a stranger to sunburn, I had surprised her with this treatment. Thankfully it works for first degree steam burns too. She wanted to spread margarine on me! She reported no blisters, I had escaped second degree burns.

Henry and the gang all kept the sauna at reasonable if hot temperature after that. We got to be friends. Henry even offered me a lot on his land to build a cabin for Marie and me.

RAISN JACK

When Dobson asked if we knew about the bootlegger he finished with "besides the homebrew that's about to explode behind the heater." "Busted." Gary and I said in unison.

"No, Emmo is a dry village but possession isn't illegal. You guys are OK for now, just don't sell any. What are you making?"

"I don't know but it's got to be better than the local stuff. We boiled the water to kill the wild yeasts and other bacteria. Plus, it's going to be almost two weeks old, most of the local stuff is less than two days. Couldn't get any malt, we thought we'd try to improve the local raisin jack. Still worried wild yeast is getting in when we burp it." I said as I pulled the white five-gallon plastic egg bucket out from behind the heater. The lid was about ready to pop off. I lifted a corner, whoosh, a gush of yeasty gas escaped. "We also aged it longer than the normal two days." I said.

"Two days is old brew for some of these guys. I don't think anything can help jack's flavor, you'll have to let me know how it comes out." Dobson added.

"It does smell a little like beer. Wish we could have found a S valve to let it breath while it was fermenting. That top gets such and arch on it, I expect it to blow any minute." I added.

After Dobson left, Gary and I decided go ahead with our Fourth of July celebration with a little raisin jack. The first glass was pretty bad.

"Needs more raisins." Choked out Gary.

"How would you know, you've never made it before. Could be wild yeast got in when we were burping it." I suggested.

"Could be this is the way it always tastes. Let's have a second glass to see if it gets better." Gary said.

At Gary's suggestion, we did and it did. The third and fourth glasses were certainly better. Finally, there was too much sediment in the glasses to allow any palatability. I picked up the glasses and weaved a course to the kitchen sink with them. I returned to the table.

"As long as I'm up, may as well take this bucket to the river and rinse it out." It was filled with the dregs of the jack.

"I have a better idea. You carry the bucket and I'll get the gas can. We can take the boat and rinse the bucket out in mid-channel." Gary slurred as he wobbled towards the door.

Is he wobbling or are my eyes crooked! Maybe I'm wobbling. Definitely think I am drunk.

Guess this shit really works. My stomach turned over. *Never again.*

We made it to the river without incident or witnesses, we thought. *I hope no one saw us. Some face of Department.* Struggling with the boat, we kept bending over to push, lost our balance, grabbed the boat for support. We avoided face plants but the boat didn't make any progress to the water. Somehow, in spite of the whirlys, and my churning stomach from too much raison jack, the boat was finally launched by a couple of giggling idiots. Gary took the outboard's tiller. I put the sediment filled bucket onto the boat's floorboards. I finished pushing the boat off, rolling rather than jumping in. Laughing, Gary accelerated in reverse jerks, keeping me off balance, and on the floorboards. As he shifted to forward, I was finally able to pull myself onto the front seat. He gave the boat full throttle, I ended up in the bilge, flat on my back. "Shit! you fucking bastard," I hollered at a hysterical Gary. I rolled over, discovered the bucket had overturned, I was coated in raisin jack sediment. Gary's laughter prevented his breathing, until he broke into a cough. Taking advantage of his indisposition, I crawled onto the middle bench. ***Proud of yourself?***

Still laughing hysterically, Gary began doing figure eights, at full throttle, making the boat jump its own wake repeatedly. Feeling sick, I slid to my knees in the bilge, hugging the gunwale, hanging my head over the side. Watching the brown water racing past, inches away from my face, finished off my stomach.

My puke joined the slipstream of air passing the speeding boat. Instead of going over the side into the water as planned. *Wow, like the spray out of a hose. Why does it move so slow? It's hitting Gary!*

Gary's victory cheer stopped almost before it started, he killed the throttled crying out "O shit. It's all over me."

I began laughing so hard I was sick again. Over the side this time. Bobbing in the middle of the river, one swearing and scooping handfuls of water trying to wash; the other laughing and puking, we made a fine picture.

Done puking. Not moving. Clean-up. Rinse bucket. I bent over the side, filling the bucket. *Need to rinse sediment out of bottom of boat; <u>better yet rinse Gary with a bucket of water!</u>* I rose from the gunwale, pulling a full bucket of water out of the river. One knee on the seat, I grabbed the rim on bucket bottom and cocked my arms back.

"Gary, you look like you could use a shower." I said.

His swearing and splashing stopped, he looked at me ready to fire. "No, please don't." A pleading look in his eyes.

His face was priceless. ***Your partners, don't do it.*** <u>*He deserves it.*</u> *Richard's right.* I didn't hurl the water. Settled for the fear on his face. I launched the water into the floorboards to rinse off the raisin jack sediment. A little spray hit Gary. Purely unintentional. We were a team again as I took my seat, Gary gently accelerated bring the water and sediment down through the floorboards. He then pulled the drain plug and everything went out the drain hole. Plug in place we returned to the beach.

"I'm sure glad you decided not to throw that water on me." Gary said.

"Hey, I thought puking on you was enough." We both walked to the house laughing.

The next morning, as I swilled coffee, before and after radio schedule, Gary came out of the bedroom grumbling about his head. I turned back to the radio, pretending to be busy, really laughing. After a pot of coffee, we thought a hot sauna and shower would improve our heads. As we walked the constant itch in between my toes began turning into pain. When I pulled my boots off, my socks were bloody. *Geez, what is this terminal athlete's foot. No more Tinactin. Should I use shower. <u>Hell yes, Alfred disinfects daily.</u>* The sauna and shower removed the protective crust that had formed and the walk home was hell. I stopped at the store on the way back but they didn't have any athlete's foot meds. *I can't stand this. Have to ask Fritz to send some.*

Back in the office, I sat down for pipe, coffee and contemplation. *Alfred uses Clorox to disinfect the showers. Should work on toes.* ***It's poisonous!*** *Dilution is the solution. Chemistry T.A. use to say that freshman year. Alfred uses a gallon in a 2 ½ gallon bucket.* ***Too much.*** <u>*Chicken.*</u> *We use half tablespoon for five gallons of drinking water. Try a cup plus three cups water.*

The chlorine odor filled the room as I prepared my cure in the rectangular plastic washbasin we used under our dish drying rack, only thing big enough for my foot. I set it down on the floor, pulled-up a chair and pulled off my shoes and socks. *Hope Gary doesn't walk-in.* I put my right foot in. "FUCK, GOD DAMN, SHIT, FUCK, HELL." I used and reused every swear word I knew, slamming my hand down on the table, trying to make it hurt worse to take my mind off the pain in my foot.

Don't break table. Pain easing. My watering eyes looked at my foot in the shaking water. The toes appeared to have turned white. I started wiggling my toes and spreading them as wide as I could. Each toe spread caused a just bearable stab of pain as the chorine reached new flesh. Finally, all the pain stopped, my breathing returned to normal. I pulled my foot out and put it on the towel I had thought to leave on the floor next to the basin. I relaxed and caught my breath.

Damn, now the left foot.

With both feet finished I walked on my heels to get my forgotten shower bag and drying washrag. Poured out the chlorinated water into the slop bucket and refilled the basin with fresh water. I then scrubbed my toes. What seemed like huge amounts of now bleached white flesh came off on the washrag. Leaving pink, tender new flesh. I pulled on clean socks and heel walked to the kitchen. Mixing up a smaller batch disinfectant which I poured into my boots and tennis shoes. Swishing around well before pouring out and leaving to dry.

I quickly got tired of heel walking, particularly after explaining why to Gary.

"Are you nuts!" He hollered, wide eyed.

"Probably, but my feet don't burn and itch, so maybe it was the right thing."

"Yeah, but you'll probably die in your sleep tonight. You can't walk on your heels till your shoes dry." Gary added.

"Yeah, guess I'll try the tennis shoes. Guess if it's just wet with chlorine, I can't catch athlete's foot again. Hope that new flesh isn't to tender." It wasn't. I had damp socks that night when I undressed but the maddening itch was gone and the shoes were almost dry. I was athlete's foot free the rest of the summer.[42]

---

[42] WHAT EVER YOU DO, DON'T TRY THIS AT HOME. MEDICAL PROFESSIONALS WHO'VE HEARD THIS STORY ARE AGREED I WAS LUCKY NOT TO SUFFER A PERMENANT INJURY.

MARIE

Our sleep was interrupted by a desperate cry for help and pounding on the office door. My bunk being closest, I jumped out of bed to see what the trouble was. I opened the door and was nearly knocked down by a someone running past me screaming for help. A young man appeared at the foot of our entrance ramp before I could turn to check on our "guest." He was quickly joined by another, then a third. The first said "We want the girl!"

So, my late-night visitor is a girl. How bad do they want her? "She doesn't seem to want you so get lost!" I said in my toughest voice.

"There's three of us!" He threatened.

"There's three of us too." *Hope Mike and Allo are awake.*

The pack huddled. The cool night air reminded me I was standing there being tough in only my white boxers. *How tough can I look?*

The pack broke their huddle, I stepped back getting ready to grab the door to slam it in their faces but they drifted off into the night. *One crisis over. Girl next?* Back inside I stepped back into the bunkroom and grabbed my jeans and t-shirt from the top bunk, quickly dressing so I would be presentable for female company.

Mike murmured from his fart sack "What's going on?"

"Three guys chasing a girl. She's in the office. Guess she needs to hide till it's safe." "Try and keep the noise down." A sleepy Mike asked.

Dressed, I padded barefoot across the dirty floor into the office. *Going to have to sweep tomorrow.* The pull-string for the light was lost in the dark. Waving my arm over the table I found it and gave a pull. Light flooded the room. The mop of black hair huddled in the corner began screaming "No! Keep them away." She turned, huddling tighter, the top of her head in the corner with her arms covering it, she kept screaming "Keep them away."

Mike called from his bunk "Shut her up." I turned the light off. *That stopped the screaming. Now what.* Carefully, since I was now night blind from the light, I took a couple of steps towards the sobbing girl/woman in the corner. *Don't get to close. You might scare her. Wonder if she is hurt? Raped? Scared for sure. Wonder how her English is? Do I need Allo to translate?*

"Hi, my name is Kim. Are you hurt?" She continued sobbing. "Your safe now. I chased those guys away. We have a spare bed if you need a place to sleep." The sobbing continued and I took a seat on the floor. *Daydreams of rescue never went this way. Scared those guys off.*

Didn't know you had it in you. *How dumb, facing three to one odds in nothing but my boxers.*

How long till Mike and Allo could help? **Kim, remember the sobbing girl/woman in the corner.**

"What's your name? You really are safe now." She seemed to exert herself and managed to choke out "Mar" barely audible her voice dropped as she finished "rie".

"Marie, is a lovely name. Are you hurt or bleeding?" *That was stupid, if she was bleeding she would be hurt. At least she's not crying. Wonder what she looks like? Stop it, you dirty old man. Sure, is dark, must be a lot of clouds tonight.*

"Your Kim?" Sob. Then she took a deep breath.

"Yes, I'm Kim. You're in the Fish& Game office. I also live here. Shall I turn on the light so we can see if your hurt?" I started to get up but she reached out, fumbling in the dark, nearly put my eye out but found my shoulders, pushing me down.

"No. No light. I'm not hurt. I got away before they touched me. They thought I should fuck them all." Marie said.

Looking down I could just make out that she was leaning over so far to hold my shoulders that her face and body were nearly on the floor. I could only see her back. *That doesn't look comfortable. Her English is as good as mine. Wonder why they thought she should fuck them?*

Or is that just a strange way of saying they wanted to rape her? Using my shoulder as an

anchor, she pulled herself out of the corner so she was sitting upright facing me. Her hands on both of my shoulders and her knees touching mine.

"Kim, is a funny name for a boy. Don't think I have ever known a Kim before." She said.

Why am I always funny? Or like a brother. "I'm named after my father's favorite book. Kim by

Rudyard Kipling. Have you heard of it or studied it in school? Usually they teach his poems "The White Man's Burden" or "Gunda Din"." I explained. *To dark to see her, even this close.*

"I don't remember those but, it's hard to remember right now." Marie started giggling loudly, uncontrollably.

"Hey, keep it down. People are trying to sleep." Mike hollered from his bed.

"Who's that?" She said in a stage whisper.

In a real whisper, I said "That's Mike. He and Allo are sleeping in the other room."

"Traded three village boys for three Kass'aks." Giggling loudly. "I might be in more trouble now than before."

Should I tell her Allo's Yup'ik? Naw. "No, you're safe. They just want to sleep." "Please shut-up." Mike called.

Giggling "Oops, better keep it down." More giggling. "Boys always want fuck."

Getting uncomfortable sitting here. Wonder if I can get her up on the chairs. I tried to get up but her hands pressed firmly down on my shoulders.

"You must stay here. You're keeping the arms away." She explained.

"What arms?" I asked.

"The ones that reach for me when light is on." Marie answered.

"Where do they come from?" I said.

"Right out of the walls." She explained.

"Are you stoned?" I said finally realizing the obvious.

Giggling, "Yes, we dropped acid. But then the boys thought it would be fun to fuck me while I was high. I didn't want to so I ran away. You saved me." She pulled herself close and kissed me.

Nice kiss. More like rescue dreams. Brilliant deduction about drugs, now what. The first aid class for drugs, said all you can do for acid is minimize external inputs and keep them safe.

Sex would kind of maximizing external stimulation. Wonder what that would be like.

"Aren't you uncomfortable on the floor?" I asked. *Negative outside stimulation.*

"Yeah, I could lay down, but want you with me, to keep me safe." Marie said.

"OK. This floor is kind of hard and dirty. How about we lay next to each other on my bunk?"

"All right. Where? Don't let the arms get me!" She fired at me.

"I won't. Let's stand-up together. We will stay away from the walls and the arms." I said. "OK" She agreed.

I squatted on the floor, putting my hands under her arm pits and helping her up. Her hands were using my shoulders as anchors but she started giggling so hard she was having trouble getting to her feet. As she moved, my hands discovered that she had warm full breasts uncontained by a bra. Covered only with some thin fabric. *Not a child. Wonder what she looks like? Feels nice. Wonder what this blouse is?* **Help her to her feet. Forget sex!**

We made it to a swaying standing position. I tried to move my arm down around her waist so we could walk beside each other. Her hands came off my shoulders, wrapped around my body as she pulled me into a face to face hug.

"Don't let go. I don't want to see." She buried her face into my chest sobbing. Filling my face with loose hair. *She's stronger, than I thought. Taller too. Nice hair.*

We stood hugging for a long time. Finally, the sobbing stopped, she seemed firmly on her feet. Her foot followed my lead, she started giggling as we slid our feet sideways, crab-walking to my bunk.

As I helped her into the bunk first, she saw the wall in the moonlight that broke through the clouds and the window. She let out a scream "Keep them away!"

"Shut that bitch up!" Shouted an angry Mike.

Mike you're not helping. We resumed our standing hug with her face in my chest muffling the renewed sobbing.

Her next scream "Keep them away." Was muffled by my body. Then she continued crying.

She finally stopped, relaxing in my arms. "Kiss me." She whispered. *What the hell.* I bent my head down to hers, our lips met, she hugged me hard as her tongue explored my mouth. She started giggling, ending the kiss. "Let's go to bed." I sat down on my bunk with her in my lap.

"You're in his bed, now shut-up bitch." Mike must be watching.

"He's mean." More giggling. Marie said.

"He just wants it quiet so he can sleep." I whispered. "Let's laydown." Struggling, we managed to both lay down while still hugging. Her back to the wall so she couldn't see the arms.

"Hmm, this is nice." She lay down, her firm hips against my crotch, her hair in my face and my arms around her chest. To my surprise she fell asleep almost as fast as her head hit the pillow.

Don't remember exhaustion coming-up as a result of LSD. She did have to run away from those three rapists. This whole thing has worn me out I fell asleep.

What's happening? Falling out of bed! O yeah, Marie is in my bed. Left arm is dead, shouldn't have left it under her. Better hang on or I'll fall on the floor. I shifted myself back onto the bed, pressing Marie between me and the wall.

"Thank you for saving me Kim." Then her lips found mine in gentle affectionate kiss.

"Hmm, are you better now?" I asked.

"Yes, I think so." She whispered. The bunk room was lighter now, our short summer night was ending.

"Acid usually lasts at least twelve hours so your probably still high." I reminded her.

"No, I'm just horny and want to show you how much you mean to me." Marie said.

"No offense, normally I would jump your bones in a minute but not when you're stoned.

You don't know what you're doing. It would be like raping you, like those others wanted to do." I explained my rejection.

Her lips hit mine again as she pushed her tongue into my mouth. She threw her leg up over my hip, using it as an anchor to allow her to pump her pelvis into mine, as her hands stroked my back. She broke the kiss to take a breath and hissed "Just fuck me. You think too much."

"I know. You'd probably be great. But you would hate me when it was over for taking advantage. I like you and would like to get to know you better." I said.

"Shut-up and fuck me!" Marie almost shouted.

"Yeah, shut-up and fuck her so we can get some sleep." Mike said from our feet where his bunk adjoined mine. Marie stopped dry humping me, "Forgot about them. Maybe we shouldn't fuck."

"Probably a good idea." I seconded.

"Just fuck her or don't but shut-up." Mike added.

Marie began giggling uncontrollably. I held her shaking body for what seemed like forever, then her breathing became deep and regular again as she fell back asleep. *She wasn't back to normal.* **Did the right thing.** <u>Probably will regret</u> I dozed off too.

What the hell, whose kissing me. I woke up to Marie gently kissing my nose and eyes. She was standing, bent over the bed. *How'd she get out without waking me?* Her tongue entered my mouth and mine entered hers as we began a long French kiss. Then she pulled up and whispered "Goodbye. Thank you very much for saving me from those guys and not fucking me. You're really sweet and brave." <u>Brave you don't know him. Old ladies always think he's sweet.</u> *Give me a break.*

"Hey, you don't have to leave yet. Stay for breakfast." I offered.

"No, I have to go. Your friends aren't very happy with me." She said.

"Please stay. They won't mind." I promised.

"Won't mine if you both just shut-up." Mike mumbled.

That didn't help. I swung my legs out of the bed and followed her to the door.

"Bye, thank you again." She gave me a quick peck on the lips.

"Can I see you again?" I asked.

Marie stopped in the doorway, the sunrise finally allowing me to see her clearly for the first time. Skin tight jeans with a tank top. Great body and legs. Pretty round Yup'ik face, surrounded by a cloud of disheveled black hair. In spite of her rumpled appearance she was a babe. She finally ended the long pause as we appraised each other.

"Yes, I'll drop-by soon." Then she turned and left. I started to follow but realized I was barefoot.

"Wait, I'll put my boots on and walk with you. Those guys still might be around." I said.

"No, I'm safe now. You've done enough." She dismissed me.

She's probably a little embarrassed by what she can remember of the night. She was probably safe; her attackers having slept off their highs. I turned and went back into the office. It was six forty-five almost time for radio schedule. I filled the coffee basket with coffee and the pot with water. I put the percolator on the stove. I turned off the alarm clock to spare Mike another interruption to his sleep. Gathered clean clothes and changed out in the office. Tired, I began another day. *Wonder how long till she comes back. Maybe I can find her.*

Probably no surprise that a bunch of single eighteen to twenty somethings thrown together by their jobs at the fish processing plants and Department of Fish and Game results in some romances. Irene was first that summer. That one ended sadly, as you have already read. Our closest physical contact was holding hands. She was trying to recover from being terribly assaulted, first by three men while at high school in Bethel. Then she was assaulted by the legal system. The prosecutor dropped all charges. Everyone knew Yup'ik girls were easy. He believed the three Kass'ak rapists. I learned a lot about sex and race discrimination from our brief time as close friends.

Next was Mary, a pretty little woman who worked on the slime line. She picked me up by flirting with me on her breaks. On our first date, after supper, she told me to shut-up, took my hand and lead me to the bedroom. Next morning during breakfast when I tried to make another date she looked at me and said "Hey, never had circumcised boy before. Just wanted to try one.

Bye." And she walked out. *Wow. Now I know what's it's like to be treated like a piece of meat.*

No wonder girls don't like it. Wonder how she knew I was circumcised? Spies in the shower?

❦

Then came Marie. Mike gave me grief for not taking advantage of opportunity when it knocked. Particularly when I wondered when Marie would be back. After four or five days of Mike's grief while we finished work on the Wahoo and did subsistence surveys in Emmo and the surrounding villages, Mike and Allo left, going upriver to finish the subsistence survey. I envied them taking a boat across Alaska on the Yukon. Mike's parting words were about Marie "You'll never see her again. A hand in the bush is worth two empty." I was alone in the office until the end of the season.

Marie turned up a day or two after they had left. Marie, with carefully combed hair, an embroidered denim jacket over a red blouse, unbuttoned enough to show little flashes of cleavage. *She would fit right in on campus. The guys would follow her with their eyes and lingering lustful thoughts. Most of the other women would be angry with her for drawing their boyfriends gaze.* "Marie, aw, I'm, aw, glad to see you." I stammered out.

She smiled, "Hi Kim, guess you really didn't expect to see me again."

Wow, the high pitched scared little girl voice is gone, she has a wonderful, what? contralto voice, full, rich, smooth. You're in way over your head Kim.

"Yes, I did. You said you'd be back. So, I hoped you would be. Ah, would you like to come in or go for a walk or something?"

"I'll come in, long walk over here." I stepped to the side, holding the door open to let her in.

Need to close the door to keep bugs out. Closed she might feel trapped. Don't latch it.

She was standing at the end of the table viewing the main room. *Wonder if she's remembering that first night.* She started taking her jacket off. I was already conveniently behind her so reached up to help her with it. *Em nice, that unbuttoned blouse gives a nice peek at those fine tits from here.*

"What are you doing?" *Can she read my mind! That voice again, going to come in my jeans.*

"I was helping you with your jacket. I'll hang it up for you." I was frozen with the jacket's shoulders in my hands.

"O" She finished shrugging out of the jacket. I turned and hung it on an empty nail next to mine in the hallway. "No-one has ever done that for me before. Your full of surprises." She said.

"No-one? My grandmother would've smacked me into next week if I didn't take a lady's coat."

Laughing, she asked "Did your grandmother live with you? My grandmother lives with us."

"Err, No, at least not the grandmother I'm thinking of; my mother's mother. Mom, my father's mother lived with us awhile but it didn't work out so she moved to an old folk's home. I'm forgetting my manners, standing here talking. Have a seat," I pulled out a chair, "would you like something to drink, coffee, tea or err, water is all I have." *Almost said me after tea. Got to watch that shit.* She pulled one out for herself, I raced around behind that one to push it in and created an awkward moment, *Forgot Charlie's wife.* as she stood looking at me an unspoken question on her face. "Ugh, I was just trying to help with your chair. Another one of those manners I was taught to do for a lady."

Sudden look of realization and she laughed "I was supposed to sit in the chair you pulled out, wasn't I?"

"No, you can sit where ever you like."

"Sorry, I've never been around a gentleman before so I'm not doing the right things." Marie said.

I blurted out "You're doing all the right things. I'm no gentleman. Just a cross-cultural mixup. What did you want to drink?" I said in desperation.

"Tea will be fine. I'll help you make it." She volunteered.

"That would be great. The kitchen is right here at this end of the room." I tried not to sound to eager.

We walked into the kitchen, I was trying not to stare at her but couldn't stop. She was looking everywhere. *Why look at a scruffy bumbling idiot?*

"You have a lot of canned bacon, ham and SPAM." She said seeing the full pantry shelves.

"Yeah, budget cuts so they sent one plane with two months supplies. Supposed to last me till I leave in September. Good thing I'm not Jewish or a Moslem." I replied.

"Why?"

"O, their faiths don't allow them to eat pork. Luckily, I'm from Iowa. We're born with a pork chop in our mouths and an ear of sweet corn in each hand. I am getting a little tired of ham though." **Shut up Kim.**

"Your confusing me, born with pork chops, what does that mean?" Marie asked.

"Sorry, you wouldn't know about Iowa, farming is the largest industry. Corn is the main crop and lots of it gets fed to pigs and cattle. I think Iowa's like first or second among the states for pork and beef production. We're kind of meat eaters as a result." I spewed out. *Can't help myself.*

"I've never seen a farm. Did you live on one?" Marie asked.

"I wish. My great grandfather did pretty well farming but then went a little crazy in his old age and would go to the bar and have mortgage burning parties. Dad ended up poor." *Quit hogging the conversation. Ask about her!*

"What is a mortgage burning party?" A puzzled Marie wondered.

Need to switch conversation to her. Women don't like to talk about you. "Most farmers have to borrow money to buy land or seed. When they couldn't get a loan from the bank, they went to great grandpa, who loaned them the money but got mortgage on their land to secure the loan. If they didn't pay the money back, he got their farm. Lots of them couldn't pay, he ended up with a lot of land and mortgages." *Simple answers, ask about her.*

"Why did you want to live on a farm?" She wondered.

Still stuck on me. "Most of the land in Iowa is owned by farmers. If you want to hunt or fish you need to get permission. If you have your own, you don't have to ask. It's not like Alaska where most land is public and open to anyone. Does your family have their land claim?" *Good segway, I hope.*

"No, the nearest land was too far away from Mountain Village. My father couldn't think what he could do with 40 acres so far away." Marie explained.

"I thought they had open areas near the villages?" I said.

"No, it was all in the middle of nowhere, what would you do there?"

"I don't know. Hope they found gold or oil. Would you like more tea?" I asked.

"No, you can if you want. I'm enjoying our talk." Marie said.

"Yes, I was a freshman in Washington last year. Should get my Associate degree in business administration this year. I hear you are at U of A."

Where did she hear that? No secrets in Emmo. "Yeah, Wildlife Management. This was my first senior year." *Quit being cute.*

"First senior year, how does that work?" Marie wondered.

"I had trouble making up my mind about a major. I was a freshman at Kansas State studying pre-vet, then Grandview Junior college back home in Des Moines, for my sophomore year as a biology major. A friend was going to U of A so I gave Wildlife Management a try and I like it.

But U of A is small school so they don't offer all their courses every semester. I have to wait until next spring to take some required courses. My second senior year." *Too much about you, get back to her.*

"Wow, seems like you have covered a lot of the country. What will you do this fall?" She asked.

"Geiger says there are some fall jobs they have trouble filling because everyone is back in school. I'm hoping to get one of those. How about you?" *Got to keep this about her.*

"When fishing is done, I'll have to go home until it is time to go back." She said unhappily.

"You don't sound too thrilled about that?" I said.

"No, I don't like it there. I don't fit in. All the boys are like those ones you chased away and my parents mostly speak Yup'ik. I only speak kitchen Yup'ik. They don't like my music, not like you're playing." Marie explained.

Forgot about the Wolfman, can still hear him. Didn't turn down radio.

"How did you know how to take care of me that night?" Marie asked.

"Nothing special. I went to a seminar they had at the U of A on first aid for drug overdoses after the Purple Jesus incident. Thought it would help me get a Student Assistant job in the dorm." I explained.

"Purple Jesus? Never heard of that." She said.

"There was a freshman mixer as part of their orientation. The punch was purple. Unknown persons spiked it with Everclear, Speed and some hallucinogen probably acid. The campus was crawling with some pretty messed up freshman afterwards. The U thought a first aid class might be good in case something like that happened again. It was mainly for Resident Advisors but I went to strengthen my resume." *Kim enough with the lectures!*

"Filling in the resume. Good idea. I need to work on mine. They keep telling us to get started but I keep putting it off. Don't really have anything to put in it." Marie said.

"You'd be surprised. I'd be happy to help you.".... Our conversation continued as I explored Marie's background. She heard more than she probably cared too about my interests in science and history. After a long while she got up and stretched. Grabbed the dirty tea cups and headed for the kitchen.

"You don't have to do that. I'll get them with the rest tomorrow." I said.

"I'm not going to wash them, just put them in the sink. Do you have a honey bucket?" "Yes, pass the bunks at the end of the hall."

"OK."

I reached over turning up the Wolfman to give her some kind of privacy, the walls were very thin. *Probably not necessary. Sure, she's use to everyone hearing toilet noise.* She walked to the sink and washed her hands with the cooling tea water from the stove.

She walked back to face me "Kim, your too much, even turning up the radio for a girl. I really came to thank you for saving me the other night." She put her arms around me and pulled me close, our lips met then her tongue pushed its way into my mouth and we began a long French kiss. When we broke, she put her hands on my shoulders and pushed me back down in the chair. Then sat on my lap, with her arms around my neck.

"Now the first kiss was for talking me down. It really helped. This is for having the courage to chase those three away." Her mouth covered mine again. *Courage? I don't have any courage. Shut-up, close your eyes and enjoy stupid.* As the kiss continued my hands started a back-rub first threw her blouse then on her warm skin, after slipping them under her top. We broke for a breath and she purred "This is for not fucking me when you had the chance." Then she went back in for my lips. Her hips started grinding in my lap, she must have noticed the hard cock she was sitting on. My hands began to explore the soft curves of her breasts.

"To soon." She whispered, our lips vibrating with her words. I backed off and found a spot in the small of her back that she really enjoyed having massaged, making her purr down in her throat as she increased the downward pressure of her lap dance. The next time my hands slipped around to cup her breasts she drove her tongue deeper into my mouth as she gently rubbed my crotch with her firm bottom. I gently tickled her hard nipples and they became even more erect.

She moved her mouth back from mine "That's enough. I better go." She gasped.

"Really. I'd like you to stay awhile longer." I said.

"I bet you would." She said getting up off my lap. "But if I stay too long, I might not leave."

Standing "That would be OK too." I said.

We continued the few steps to the door holding hands. I stopped at her jacket and got it down holding it open "Here don't forget this you'll get cold."

Laughing "You really are something else. I French kiss you while doing a lap dance and let you handle my tits, you're ready to walk me home. Even though your hard on is about to break your zipper." She stroked my hard cock. "Other boys would have thrown me on the bed saying "time to fuck you prick teaser". Guess you must be a gentleman." *Who me? What's happening?*

She lead me by the hand into the bedroom..

"Tiger, I didn't think you'd ever come." Marie's tiny nose was touching mine. Her black hair making a tent out of our heads. Our hot gasping breaths filling the space with heat and humidity.

"I didn't hurt you, did I?" *Do like Tiger but don't want to hurt the girl I love.*

"No, don't think I ever had so many organisms. No one else ever let me be on top. I like it but that top bunk is in the way. You did wear me out." Marie whispered into my lips.

"I didn't want it to end. You're the best ever." *She's only number two.*

"Hmm. That's nice." She said.

We both quickly recovered and the night was too short.

⚜

"Where are you going?" I said in the morning. Her quiet dressing had woken me.

"Home to get some rest." Marie said.

"I should walk you home." *So, I know where it is.*

"Your sweet but get back in bed. I'll be alright." She said.

"Where are you staying?" I asked.

She bent over and kissed me. Then pushed me back down on the bed. "Bye I'll see you soon."

Why is where she staying a secret? Probably shouldn't ask. I could follow her. Nah that would be weird. Thoughts running through my brain as I followed her to the door so I could be near her as long as possible. *Maybe shouldn't latch it in case she changes her mind. No, that won't happen. Tiger, you probably screwed up again. To rough and she doesn't want to see you again. I'll find her at work at the Coop. She has to know I love her and can be a Teddy bear.*

I did see her again the next day and the next.

The summer chum fishery closed. I was surprised there were no complaints this time. Everyone was ready to go pick berries before the fall chum salmon fishery began. The processors closed the tent camps and laid off the extra workers. I was enjoying the closure, reading in the middle of the afternoon. Every now and then wondering what happened to Marie with the reduction in workers? She changed the subject when I asked.

What was that. Sounds like a knock on the door. Really soft. Better go see. Maybe Marie!

I opened the door. Marie's back was to me as she was about to step off the entry ramp and leave.

"Wait. I'm here. I barely heard your knock." She turned, there was a very uncertain look on her face.

"I wasn't sure I should come." Marie whispered.

"Why not? I'm happy to see you." I said as I reached her, gently taking her hand.

"No, I shouldn't have come." She was looking at the ground shaking her head NO.

<u>*Just lead her in.*</u> *No, that's not right. Give her a hug. If she'll let you? Wonder what is wrong?"* I let go of her hand and put my arms, awkwardly around her, since I was standing above her on the ramp and my being taller forced my arms more around her neck and head. I held her loosely, my arms on top of her shoulders, reassuringly I hoped. "I really do like you.

Come in, I'll slip my boots on and we can go for a walk. You can always leave." *Give her time to think. Explain?.*

"OK" she whispered. Clearly still thoughtful and uncertain. She stepped forward and I slid my arm around her waist. We walked up the ramp slowly, side by side.

"I've missed you." I said.

"It's only been two days. I was working. I needed to think, about you." She said.

"Good things I hope." *Try to follow her lead. Try not to say I love you. Too soon.*

"Yes, nice things." She sat down. "We don't need to go for a walk. I heard you were asking for me."

"That didn't scare you I hope?" I said.

"No, I thought it was nice." Marie said.

"You'll probably think I'm silly but I think I've fallen in love with you." *There you said it.*

<u>*Now you'll really be history. Why can't you keep your mouth shut?*</u>

The expected laughter didn't happen, "Pretty fast don't you think." She said.

"Yes and no. We have spent a lot of time together recently. I became very protective of you that first night. Our long talks have been great. The sex too. I'm yours to keep or throw away." *In for a penny in for a pound. Stupid, she'll dump you for sure now.*

Marie smiled leaned over and kissed me. "Well Tiger, I think you should slow down a bit." "OK, would you like tea or a pop?" I said cheerfully. *Mood is getting a little dark.*

"You never have pop?" She said in surprise.

"I splurged. Bought a six pack of Coke, I think you said it was your favorite. State won't let me buy it."

"Why's that?" Marie asked.

"It's on the prohibited luxury list. Gary and I decided the list was written by someone in Juneau who couldn't imagine there was any place without running water."

"That was nice of you." She said as she rose to help herself. I was quicker and pulled one out of the cooler. *Wish I knew what was happening.*

We talked, put together a Spaghetti-O bacon supper. A recipe I concocted out of the abundance of supplies. We continued talking with the radio providing background music. She deftly put off a couple of advances I made, so our touching was limited occasional kisses or hugs. As the evening wore on she started becoming less vivacious and more nervous and thoughtful. She brushed off my what's the matter questions. Finally, she said "I had better go." *Shit, no sex tonight. Doesn't matter if this is what it takes to keep her.*

"Can I please walk you home tonight." I begged.

She started sniffling, "I don't have anywhere to go tonight."

Confusing. They must have closed the tent camp. Where was she going? She knows she's welcome. "Huh, this isn't anywhere but your welcome to stay. There are plenty of spare bunks and I promise to keep my hands to myself."

"You would too, wouldn't you? Don't think I've ever known a boy like you." Her face went from fighting off tears, to a smile and ended in a thoughtful serious look.

"You probably have but he was the kid you ignored, who would do anything you asked but was too shy to ask you out."

"Is that what happened to you?" Marie asked.

"Yep, but I did finally start asking. Rarely had more than one date. Until this beautiful girl who needed help burst through the door in the middle of the night. I got to know her well enough to be comfortable with her." *Good job. You didn't use the L word. Thanks, felt like a lie.*

"I'll go." She said getting up and heading for the door.

"Wait, where? Let me put my boots on. I'll help." *What's she going to do sleep in an empty fish smoker?*

As she opened the door, "I don't need any help. You don't need boots. They said I can work fall chums if I'm here and have a place to stay. Can I stay with you?" She blurted out.

"Of course!" I answered.

She turned and walked down the ramp. *I said she could stay. Where she's going?* I stepped out on the ramp to call to her. She stopped at the bottom of the ramp, bent down, pulling a small suitcase and a pack stuffed to overflowing out from under the ramp.

"Won't you get in trouble?" She asked.

"No. They aren't even sending another plane until they pick me up in September. No one will know." *Regnart almost bragged about the guy in Unalakleet living with a girl. Who cares, wonder what could happen.*

Marie moved in. She passed on sleeping alone in one of the spare bunks. Thought it was funny when I started making one up for her. Remembering the space limitations of our first couple of nights, I pulled the top bunk off my bunk. Our "new" bed made our vigorous sex life much easier. We both did our jobs, at least until she got laid off when the Coho run dwindled away. She didn't want to go home for the last three weeks and I didn't want her too. When I spoke of love or marriage or transferring to the U of A, she always changed the subject. This troubled me, otherwise I was so happy I didn't think much about it. She left for her parents in Mountain Village planning to spend a couple of days at the end of the first week of September, before returning to school. I wrote to her daily. I only received one of the preaddressed postage paid postcards I had given her when she said she wasn't much of a writer. It gave me the phone number of her dorm. I called between planes from Bethel, Anchorage and Fairbanks. She was never at her dorm. Finally, when I called from the Fairbanks Airport as I was transferring from tagging salmon in Rampart to the subsistence survey in Tanana. I reached her roommate, who very unhappily told me Marie had stuck her with telling me, Marie had moved out to live with her boyfriend. I wasn't to write or call anymore. I cried on the plane from Fairbanks to Tanana, "Lemon Tree" became song always playing in my head.

❧

Fifteen years passed. I was now the Area Management Biologist for the Kuskokwim Area stationed in Bethel. The Field Administrative Assistant for the office was going on maternity leave. She and I were selecting her temporary replacement. The final five selected by headquarters in Juneau were not very impressive. The first had failed Vera's typing test and scored very poorly on her interview.[43] The second was in Barrow Alaska. While he was outstanding in his phone interview, references and application. The budget didn't even have the money for an airplane ticket for him, let alone to move his stuff from Barrow. The third and fourth were well known local unemployment scammers. Did the job well enough to be employed long enough to requalify, then screwed up so badly they had to be fired. Then they collected unemployment.

Vera, the Field Office Administrator[44], was giving the office skills test to the fifth. I was reviewing her application, that at least looked promising. "Hi Kim." A rich contralto voice shattered my concentration and transported me back in time and space fifteen years to Emmonak. I turned in my chair, Marie, stood leaning languidly against my office door frame, smiling. Our eyes met briefly and she stood erect "How have you been? I'm here for the job interview."

Come back. You have a job to do. Your happily married. *But there's so much I want to ask.* **Tough, stick to the script.** "Hi, come in and have a seat. I've prepared a set of questions I ask in each interview and score the

---

[43] At that time hiring procedure required that the interviewer prepare a set of questions. With values, one through five, to ask every interviewee. You weren't to stray from the questions to avoid potential law suits.

[44] Forgive me for using the title but when I first took the A.B. job the position was a Clerk/Typist II. Which didn't fit the duties at all. I was one of several A.B.'s who worked to get the office position upgraded. Since there wasn't a job description that fit HQ finally wrote and created the F.O.A. positions.

answers. That way everyone gets treated the same." "That sounds like a good system." Marie answered taking a seat.

"Not my idea but Juneau's. I have found interviews are easier since I took the hiring class and started using it." I looked down at the scrip. "Guess we can skip introductions, err, since we know each other."

"Yes, I think so." Marie said sitting straight in her chair with a smile. Hands folded politely in her lap. *All business. Still beautiful, waist is a little thicker.* I continued through the scrip[45].

Only hitting one little snag.

"Do you anticipate any difficulties in keeping our eight until four thirty workdays?"

"I have a son, thirteen, he comes first. If something came up that he needed me I wouldn't be here. But unless he got sick at school it shouldn't be a problem." She answered.

*Thirteen, 1972 minus 1986, fourteen. Not mine. Pretty quick after we broke-up. **Interview!*** "Of course, family always comes first. Even temps get some sick leave but try and call. If you get the job." *Still interviewing not hiring.* I moved on to the next question. We finished and I stood up and walked her to the office door. "It was nice seeing you again. I'll call to let you know about the job, one way or the other."

"It was nice seeing you and I'm glad things have gone so well for you." Marie said.

I called her last employer in Seattle, checking her references. "We were so sorry to lose her.

I offered her quite a raise to get her to stay but her husband's death really hit her hard and she had to leave."

"Her husband's death?" ***Looking for gossip isn't professional.***

"Yes, he was a crane operator, I think, killed when the crane collapsed or something. I'm glad to hear she's looking for work again. She must be recovering."

Sounds like wonder woman from his recommendation. Don't think I need to call any of these earlier ones.

Vera came to the office with the results of her hands-on test. "She's perfect, I think, she's the one you want. You want me to call and tell her?"

---

[45] Sorry the questions have completely slipped my mind.

"OK, err, thanks, no I better think about it overnight. Right now, I think your right." I replied.

OK, so how do you tell Marsha your hiring the first woman you ever lived with? You don't, dummy. That's not right. **Should tell her.** *Take the five files home and ask for her help. This is what she does. She's a better judge than you. That's the ticket.*

During supper Marsha asked if we'd found a replacement for Vera. The question I was waiting for.

"I'm not sure. We're down to the final four, since one guy is in Barrow. Ron says no budget for a move. I brought everything home. You know more about this kind of work than I do, I'd like you to look over the apps and give me your opinion."

"You hardly need my help. What does Vera say?" Marsha asked.

"She picked one but I'd like to see if you pick the same one." I said.

"OK, I'll do it while you do the dishes." Marsha trapped me.

"Rats, got me. Wish the herring crew hadn't told you I can do dishes." I whined.

"I'm glad they did." She said.

Supper over and the dishes washed, I put the last one in the drying rack. I walked into the living room. *She is so pretty. Sitting on the couch, one file in her hand three on the floor. Looks done.* "You still reading that one?"

"I was checking it again. She's obviously the right one, the others don't even come close.

Unless you know something, I don't." Marsha said.

Sitting down next to her and putting my arm around her waist I said "Yep, remember way back when we told each other about all our past lovers."

Pulling away a little she said "Wish I never done that, you're always bringing those guys up."

Pulling her back in, "It's your turn to tease this time. Remember I told you about Marie, the girl I lived with in Emmonak."

"Sort of." She said furrowing her brow in thought.

"Well that's her app in your hand." I announced.

"Really!" She looked down at the app in the open file.

What's she looking for there isn't a space for "Lived with person doing the hiring."

"Vera doesn't know, of course, and that's who she picked. If it wasn't for our past, I would picked her too, but I wasn't sure if you would be happy with me working with a former lover." "You mean if I said not to hire her you would pick one of these others?" She asked.

"Yes, that's what I mean." I said.

"You'd really do that? It's not fair to her. You should know by now that all I ask is you be honest with me. You want someone else, I'll leave. Just don't want any sneaking around." She said seriously.

Hugging her tightly, if awkwardly, we were shoulder to shoulder, I answered "I thought you'd be OK with it. Marie was very business-like during the interview, making it clear, with her body language, she wasn't depending on our past. If hired, she and I won't discuss the past.

Even though there are a lot of questions. **The answers "Don't mean shit."** *Thank you, Mr. Natural.*

I hired Marie and she did a great job. We both were friendly but business-like, although once the office manager did say "Marie really protects you, treats you special. Is there a reason?" I started to ask what she meant, **Richard** stopped me. I said I didn't know what she meant. By the time Vera's maternity leave was over the staff wanted to keep Marie. But Marie didn't want to stay, which was a good thing since the job was Vera's, unless she quit. Marie received a large settlement as a result of her husband's death and didn't need to work anymore. She was eager to go, as she told me a few times towards the end, when she was checking on when Vera would return.

Vera came back, continued doing a great job. Marie went off to her life of leisure.

Housekeeping The raucous bell on the alarm clock shattered my sleep. *Damn, fucking thing.* **It gets you up.** *Wonder if there are less annoying windup alarms. There's my beautiful girl. Wonder what time she finally got in. These extra shifts sure are cutting into my sex life. If there's time for a quickie. Naw, let the poor girl sleep.* I got the radio warming up, coffee cooking, and took a break.

I listened to Fritz call the weir. The only Kuskokwim camp still operating. Then it was my turn, the last camp on the Yukon. "KE6628 Emmonak, KE6628 Emmonak this is KE6628 Bethel calling."

To hell with procedure, FCC not listening on Saturday. Tired of all these KE6628s. I'll never forget that number. "This is Emmonak go ahead Bethel."

"Grouchy this morning. Stand-by for Geiger."

Geiger! Shit I don't have the verbals yet. Wasn't supposed to have them till eight. What's happening?

"KE6628 Emmonak this is Bethel." Geiger's deep voice came in. "Are you ready for a news release?"

I turned the radio log, legal sized yellow ruled pad, to a fresh page. "Roger Bethel."

"The harvest guideline for fall chum salmon in Districts 1, 2 and 3 has been taken. The total catch is; you fill in the totals from the verbals, got that?"

This is new, guess he trusts me. "Roger"

"which is; you do the math, over the harvest guideline of 250,000 fall chum salmon. District 1, 2 and 3 will remain closed until August 25 when commercial fishing will reopen for Coho salmon." That's it. Be sure a clean copy is in the next package of fish tickets you mail." "Roger"

"Emmonak, put a package in the mail for you," *Getting tired of that too. Why the hell won't the FCC let them use my name.*, "do you need anything else?" Fritz was back, having switched with Geiger.

Marie had just padded into the kitchen in one of my shirts, long brown legs, tousled hair, my shirt never looked so good. *Nope got everything I need right here. No, don't say that on the air you smug bastard.* "No Bethel I'm good. A little tired of ham with bacon." I said.

"Aren't we all, but it's SPAM for lunch again today. Bethel out." Fritz replied. "Sorry to wake you." I hung up the mike. *This talking to Bethel and myself is confusing, probably need to stop.* I crossed the room and slipped up behind Marie, my hands under her/my shirt filled with her warm breasts. My crotch pushing against her firm warm ass.

"Down Tiger. Sorry, I'm going in to work. We barely finished Wednesdays fish before yesterdays started coming in. Don't worry I'll fuck your brains out when this is over. Toast burning! Let go." I loosened my grip so she could grab the toast off the pyramid toaster that covered one burner. Marie got the four pieces on to a plate then tried to pull away as I once again tightened my hug, while fondling her tits. "Kim, let go!"

"OK, would you like me to fry some SPAM or bacon to go with your toast?" I asked as she stepped away.

"That would be nice. That sandwich you brought me for lunch yesterday was a lifesaver.

Also made the other girls jealous." Marie said.

"Hmm, I don't know why. You could do a lot better than me." *That was stupid. Don't put yourself down, even if it's true.* Marie made a thoughtful humming sound threw her mouthful of toast. I served up some barely warm SPAM. Then started on a SPAM sandwich for her lunch. She gobbled up her food, washing it down with coffee, then padded into the bedroom to get dressed before I finished the sandwich. To escape my randy intentions, no doubt.

"Do you want a ride?" *Nice double meaning.*

"No, processors will be calling in their verbals. You need to be on the radio. Bye, see you later." We kissed and she was out the door.

Nice, she's learning my job as well as me. Breakfast and the radio. Hey, that was my shirt she wore to work. Have to scrounge up some quarters for a load of laundry. Wonder if my bank statement will be in the package from Bethel? Wonder if the state has paid me yet? Seven weeks for that first check was tough. Suppose the second will take as long?

Processor's verbals confirmed what Geiger expected. It was another record catch and the harvest guideline was exceeded by a record amount. I finished up my news release. I sat back with a fresh cup of coffee and a fresh pipe. *Geiger knew that would happen when he allowed the period. Still be Hell, to pay on the radio tonight. Probably another public meeting. Survived the first, suppose a second won't hurt me. I hope. They don't show this part of the job on Wild Kingdom. Guess this is why they require Speech. Starting to think they might need to require a lot more from the sociology department. Better get these delivered.*

News release delivery was more than routine. No one argued, just cold shoulder. No one wanted to talk. As I crossed to the Bering Trader. I decided they didn't want to repeat uselessly asking for an extension. The bookkeeper at the Trader already had their fish tickets and handed them to me. "Get a cup of coffee. The boss wants to see you." He disappeared into the ship. I went into the galley and sat down with a mug of joe. He should be happy. Won't run out of cans for Cohoes. It would be interesting to go out to sea on one of these. Wonder if I could hitch a ride to Seattle when this is all over.

"Hi Kim. Thanks a lot. Glad the fall chum season is over. Thought you should hear that from one person. Took an inventory after I got the fish count. I think I'm just going to have enough cans to fill the Coho contract. Going to have to ride the guys to be really careful rolling them not to ruin any. But I think we'll make it. I should get back down to the line. Anything you need?"

"No. Thanks for the thank you. Won't hear many of those. Of course, I had nothing to do with it."

"Pass it along to Geiger when you get a chance. Take care. Bye."

"Bye." *That's that. Back to Emmo. Forgot to ask about Seattle. Maybe I'll do bacon for lunch. Getting tired of SPAM. Record catch and record price. Should be full pockets and happy fishermen instead of all this grumping. Guess there's never enough money. Not many like Charlie.*

❦

Back at the office, I was starting to add up Bering Trader fish tickets when a young man unknown to me came in and gruffly said "Here's AC's tickets.". *Where's Ed? Everyone's early but not very happy. Wonder if the Coop has theirs? Have to check after lunch.*

Back to the Olivetti. Adding up the two companies' tickets didn't change things, in fact the Bering Trader was a little low on their verbal. After lunching on a whole pound of fried bacon, I packed up my shower gear and laundry, walked up to the post office and Coop, planning to shower on the way back. By the time I reached the post office I was wishing I had taken the skiff. Couldn't seem to go ten feet without being stopped and asked why there wasn't an extension. The good news at the post office was there was a nice thick manila envelope from Bethel. At the Coop I stepped into the inner office and found the lovely bookkeeper working on her pile of pink fish ticket copies. I waited quietly, watching her work, which was an easy thing to do, she finished the stack. I coughed. She jumped.

114

"I'm sorry, I was trying not to break your train of thought. I know all about fish ticket brain." "Do you dream about these damn things too?" She asked.

"Yeah, had a couple like that. The lost ticket one is the worse."

"Tell me about it. You didn't come to talk about fish ticket brain, did you?" She asked.

"Only indirectly. Everyone else has turned theirs in. Thought you might have yours too, so I can get a head start." I answered.

"Yes, there ready. Here they are. Save's you and I a trip on Sunday." She said.

"Will you miss the over time?" I asked.

"Don't get any. Do you get over time?" She asked.

"No, I was just hoping someone did. This salaried business[46] gets old, but I do still get paid during the closures for twiddling my thumbs."

"Goodbye, I have work to do." She answered.

"OK. Bye, back to fish tickets."

Curious, it has gotten much easier to talk to women, especially pretty ones since sex started. Must be a confidence thing. Interesting. I continued pondering imponderables all the way to the shower and laundry. Busier than normal. Can't wait for fish opening to cut down the crowd. "Hi. Mr. Redfox, looks like business is good today."

"Yes, no fishing, lots of money. There's room for you."

I enjoyed Alfred. He worked hard at the plant and took great pride in it. He also didn't give me any flak about the fishery, even though he was a fisherman too. I striped down and walked past all the showers my eyes averted, and into the sauna. Seemed like I had just arrived at the beginning of the fire bath. Only one of the old men I knew was there. The rest were new.

The temperature wasn't hot yet. My arrival caused a discussion in Yup'ik. Henry invited me up to sit with him on the top bench. One of the newbies started hitting the rocks with water. Henry gave me a knowing grin. It got hotter and hotter. The little thermometer on the wall was

---

[46] Salaried was not strictly true. For legal reasons, IRS always got the blame, we were hourly. But we filled out and signed timesheets for a five day eight to four thirty regular time workweek. Saturday was overtime for seven and a half hours. Our actual work/off hours were not recorded.

pegged. My skin was burning and I was breathing threw my wet wash cloth. Henry had his wet grass bundle to protect his lungs. A newbie had already left letting in a rush of cool air that gave a moments relief. Henry slipped down a bench. I was alone on the top bench. *We're up to your dare.* The guy on the lowest bench continued throwing water to raise the temp. Not long after Henry, descended another newbie left the second-tier bench for the lowest level as another had dropped to the floor. I took his place. Henry and I were alone on the second-tier. With regular glances at me the fiend with the water continued. He was too eager to make steam and actually cooled the rocks so badly the water just ran through to the floor. He realized his mistake and backed off to let the rocks heat up. Another newbie left. The cool air when the door opened was marvelous. The relief was short lived. The rocks were hot and another cloud of steam arose. The fiend had joined two others on the floor. Henry and I exchanged a coordinating glance and slipped together to the lowest tier of benches. The fiend continued. His two remaining companions on the floor gave up fleeing out the door. The fiend created one more cloud of steam and fled, unable to stand his self-made hell. The elder and I sat quietly for a few minutes. As the heater gave off ticking sounds as it cooled. I noticed for the first time that the cedar safety fence around the heater was charring on the inside. It hadn't been designed for Yup'iks, whose first modification had been to remove the thermostat that controlled the maximum temp.

"Girlfriend good?" Henry asked.

A little startled "Yes, she great."

"Going marry?" He asked.

"We're thinking about it." *To many words. Can't breathe that deep. Is Marie thinking about it?*

"Good.".…. "Forty acres"… "other side Kwiguk"… "let you have twenty"… "if marry".

… "For cabin.". Henry's sentence was broken by the need to breath cool air through his wet- grass.

"Thank you. won't be, for a while yet, she doesn't know." I chopped out, between draughts on my rolled-up washrag.

"She good girl, she marries." He assured me.

Statement of fact or if she doesn't marry not a good girl? "Hope so." *Wow, that's a surprise. I don't even know his last name. There aren't any houses on the other side. Have to commute by boat and skis. If I live here probably get snow-go. Even my inner voice is starting to use Yup'ik English slang? Jargon? English Yup'ik? Have to find linguist when I get back to campus. Not sure what I would do in winter? Trap mink and muskrats, I guess. There he goes.*

The cool air will let me last a few more minutes. I'll show those guys. Don't think Marie wants to live in a village. Standing I almost collapsed. My head seemed unattached to me. Grabbing the door handle to stay upright, I pulled it open, still using the door for support I swung it shut behind me. A few staggering steps to the nearest shower stall, which wasn't empty. Grabbing the door frame for support I said "Excuse me." Then pulled myself to the next stall which thankfully was empty. I collapsed to the floor. As I had seen so many of my fellow maqivivik (steam bath) users do in the past. ***You swore never again.*** *They dared again.* Still stupid.

I was the only man in the laundry when I emptied my machine into the dryer. I read my book with Yup'ik chatter in the background. I became a source of entertainment when I began sorting and folding our clothes. My struggle folding Marie's panties was a real source of laughter.

⁂

Back at the office, my red face cooling, I once again started the routine of processing the latest batch of fish tickets. I finished the tickets just in time to have a final for Fritz at 4:30 PM which seemed to surprise him. He said "Nice job." I just hopped Geiger thought so too. Marie missed supper. But it was only another ham fry up. I covered a plate with a paper towel. Turned on the radio and opened a book. She stumbled in about 10:30.

"Tough day, babe?" I asked.

"Last one till Cohoes. I just want to go to bed." She answered "Me too!" I said jumping up.

"No, to sleep." She replied, a little alarmed.

"I know. I joke." I said.

Laughing on her way to the bedroom. "You don't say it right. I jokes. But I don't. Good night."

⁂

Next morning after radio schedule I stepped out the door, coffee in hand to check the weather. I almost stepped in the latest item in our meat swap. A heavy white plate with a piece of almost black meat. *What's that? Beluga? Hope Marie knows.* Picking it up I went back inside and put it in the cooler. Sat down to read and drink coffee but instead remembered how this all started.

After the subsistence crew left I had stepped out to cool off after a hot session with Marie and nearly stepped in a plate with a roast on it. Didn't quite look like beef but Marie identified as moose. She was thrilled, already tiring of Sapgetteo's and ham. The AC Fisheries manager told me a cow moose had been shot the night before up by where the Kwiguk emptied out of the Yukon. The roast was my share. This raised an ethical problem for me, did I report the poached moose or eat the evidence. The meat wasn't really evidence and I wasn't able to find out anything else about the poaching except what, when and where. The who was a secret. The four Ws that they taught us in deputation class. I reported the three Ws I had on radio schedule and enjoyed a delicious moose stew with Marie. Quite a treat after all the ham and bacon. At Marie's suggestion I left a canned ham on the washed plate the next night. After that we began an infrequent exchange of pork products for ducks and geese.

Marie stepped out of the bedroom and helped herself to coffee.

"Good morning sunshine, take a look in the cooler, the elves left us some meat I don't recognize." I greeted her. She squatted down and opened the cooler, peering sleepily in.

Slamming the lid closed she simultaneously said "Yuk, damn seal. I hate that stuff." "I've never had it before. I'd like to try it." I said.

"Then you'll cook it yourself while I'm somewhere else." Marie swore.

"I don't think that's in the Yup'ik Wife's handbook." I smarted off.

"I'm not your wife, I don't cook, eat or even smell that damn seal meat while it's cooking.

Fuck you and your Handbook."

"Your beautiful when your angry." I said taking her in my arms. "You don't have to cook it. I'll fix it for lunch while you're at the shower.

"Sounds like a good plan. What's for breakfast?" She asked and I went to work on my Heinlein bacon fat recipe.[47]

---

[47] In one of Heinlein's novels he mentions putting dry bread into bacon fat to make a meal out of it. I added a couple of eggs to the scramble and since bacon was plentiful served the strips on the side. Good stuff.

Marie was doing a load of laundry and taking a shower latter and I fried-up the seal. I can't really recommend it. Of course, may have been my preparation or palate. It's not awful but it's very dense and chewy. With an odd flavor that I can't really compare to anything.

With minor variations this was the way we lived in August that year. Marie left during the first week of September to return to school.

TAGGING SALMON

The Wein Air flight to Fairbanks was open seating. Window seats seemed to be going fast but I snagged one of the last ones left. Sank into my seat and stared out at the runway. *Only one postcard from Marie. Two tries to the phone number and missed her both times. Wonder if the Sharps will mind me arriving unannounced at nine. Probably be OK, they're like a second family. Wonder who'll be my partner on subsistence survey? Hope he's not a jerk.*

"How'd Spider Boy come out?"

I looked up from my thoughts of the future to find Ron Regnart, our Regional Supervisor, putting a small bag into the overhead bin. *Spider Boy, the radio drama we were listening to when Director Rosier walked into the office in Emmo. Regnart told him to "Be quiet, sit down, Spider Boy." The look on the Director's face was priceless. Don't think he was used to commands.*

"Hi Mr. Regnart, predictably he caught the bad guy." I said after a moment of hesitation.

"OK if I join you? I keep telling you it's Ron." He said sitting down.

"I'll try and remember. Dad taught me to be respectful of my superiors."

"You've been alone in Emmo for a couple of months now." He replied.

"Err, I wasn't alone. Had a lot of friends there." *Best not to mention Marie.*

"That's good. Probably part of the reason you did so well. Geiger said you're the best fish ticket editor he's ever had. He's been able to use your numbers to check the computer runs for mistakes. Hasn't had to retabulate everything himself." Ron said to my surprise.

"Really, I thought I was doing terrible." I said, remembering Geiger's stone face and short conversations.

"He didn't tell you? That's Mike, I've been trying to coach him on giving people at-a-boys.

We need to see him on vacation. He evidently really lets loose then." Ron said.

"He does? They call him stone face in the village."

"You won't believe this but during one of his vacations, I get a call in the middle of the night. "Senior Regnart", a voice says, "Do you know a Senior Michael Geiger?" He said in a hooky Mexican accent.

I say "Yes he works for me."

The voice comes back "So he has a job and isn't a vagrant?" I tell him Mike has a job and asked "What is this about?

The voice says "There's been a little bit of trouble here and we needed to check on Senior Geiger."

I ask "Does he need bail money or something?"

With the accent "No, just needed to confirm his job. Audios."

Geiger got back on time with a nice tan. Never would tell me what happened. Don't tell him I told you about this." Ron closed.

"OK, I won't but that sure doesn't sound like the Geiger I know. What do you mean he's using my numbers to check the computer runs?" I asked.

"All the fish tickets go to Juneau. The key punch gals enter them into the mainframe computer down there. Then they print it out and send it back to the ABs for proof reading.

Which is a real pain and unless there's a huge error on something you can't tell if there's a mistake, without going through the tickets one at a time. But your numbers were so accurate if they disagree with the computer Mike uses them for reentry. In the past he used to have to go through the fish tickets. How did you get so good at it? Usually the fish ticket editors are so sloppy the computer run is more likely to be right." Ron explained and asked.

"Ugh, guess it's cause last summer I worked as a pay roll clerk for Green Construction.

You don't want to screw-up those guys' hours. They know to the penny what they have coming.

If it's different, you better be able to show them where their mistake is. Their system had the same crosscheck as the fish ticket system. The column up the side has to equal the row across the bottom or you've messed up. Sometimes took a while to figure out why they didn't match, but I figured that's what I was getting paid to do." I said.

"Different attitude than most seasonals. They don't care if the rows and columns equal each other. Geiger said you were the same way with your AWL samples. Made more sample goals than anyone else who has ever done it." He told me.

I sort of looked at my lap. *Wow, other people sure must be lazy.* "Thanks."

"You need to learn to blow your own horn more. No one will blow it for you. Keep up the good work. You have a future here. You going back to U of A this fall?" Ron asked.

"No. Geiger choose me to finish the subsistence survey and take the Wahoo back to Emmo.

Guess it was his at-a-boy." I said.

"What about your degree?" He said.

"U of A doesn't have all their classes every semester. Last year was my official senior year but I still have some required courses to finish, but they are all spring semester courses. I couldn't think of anything I would rather do than float the length of the Yukon so I jumped at the chance when Mike offered." *Spending the whole semester with Marie in Seattle was tempting but I can survive till I get there in a few weeks.*

"What will you do after that? I don't think we have any jobs that run later." Ron queried.

"I met a girl this summer, who's in college in Seattle. Probably will visit her." I said.

"You really weren't alone all that time in Emmo." He said winking.

Turning red, I looked at my lap. "Yeah, she's pretty special."

"That's nice. You'll be coming back to work for us next summer?" Ron asked.

"If you'll have me, of course with a degree I'll probably be looking for a permanent job, but if I'm still looking, guess I can look from Emmo as well as a tent in Fairbanks. Phone calls will be harder." I said.

Ron laughed saying "Yep, at least you'll have a roof over your head."

We were lucky, the flight was being flown by the pilot who played harmonica really well and liked to entertain. He announced his first number and let go.

"Only in Alaska would a pilot do that." Ron commented between numbers.

"Yea, last summer I went to Sitka for a wedding. I drove to Haines, then flew to Sitka. The Haines Airport is even less than the Bethel's. I'm sitting on this twin Otter full of blue haired tourists off a cruise ship, except for a couple of lumberjacks towards the back sleeping off the night before. Take off time came and went, still no crew. People were discussing what to do.

One lumberjack gets out of his seat saying "Damn airline never has been able to run on time." The other one closes the passenger door, as his partner stomps up the aisle announcing "I'll fly the plane."

I figured out it was the pilot giving the tourists a little show. Not sure they needed it, most were already shocked at the idea of flying in something with propellers and too small for a stewardess. He fired up the engines and off we went. Thought my fellow passengers were going to die. As they listened to him do all the required announcements they started to figure out the joke. He gave them a great story to tell when they got home."

Ron bought us beers from in-flight service. It's a pretty short hop from Anchorage to Fairbanks in a 737 so we both had to chug about half a can when they cleaned the cabin for landing. At the gate Ron was greeted by none other than Carl Rosier, Division Director, of Spider Boy fame.

"I'll buy you both a drink after you pick-up your luggage." Carl said.

"I better a call to be sure I have a bed tonight. I don't have much. I'm sure I can pick-up Ron's luggage with mine and meet you both in the bar." *He travels light as I recall.* <u>*Peons on*</u> *should be peons.*

Ron gave me his ticket jacket with the luggage claim stapled to it. "I'll get my rent a car and after our drink I'll drop you wherever you need to go."

"That works for me." I left the two of them and headed for the luggage claim. Luggage wasn't out yet so I went to the bank of pay phones and called the Sharps.

"Hi Bert. It's Kim Francisco."

"How and where are you?" Bert asked.

"I'm fine, had a great summer in Emmonak. I'm at the Fairbanks Airport. My boss's boss and his boss want to buy me a beer, then they'll drop me off. I was hoping I could crash at your place tonight. Think I'll be flying out to somewhere on the Yukon tomorrow." I said.

"Of course, you can stay. Back door is open. I'll see you in the morning over sourdough pancakes. Better let you get back to this executive meeting." Bert teased.

"Thanks, that will be great." Betsy, Bert's wife, makes these sourdough pancakes with wild blueberries that were amazing. Huge, thick, but still light. One was a meal but like most people I couldn't stop at one and usually managed three which filled you for the rest of the day. Dreaming of sourdough pancakes I found a spot on the far side of the luggage claim conveyor belt. This side, where unclaimed luggage went back into the mysterious luggage handling area before going around and coming out again with freshly added luggage was always almost deserted. Where the conveyor belt came out on the other side seemed to be packed with people standing shoulder to shoulder, two or three deep trying to claim their bag as soon as it came out. Never made sense to me to crowd in and fight for my luggage. My pack with sleeping bag rolled and strapped to the top came out while I was watching for the other half of Ron's claim ticket. It was on a green army duffle bag. I pulled it off, grabbed my pack and put it on. Then grabbed the duffle bag and walked to the bar. At the door, it looked like a second baggage claim area.

There was a huge pile of bags behind a little desk, where I supposed sometimes a hostess stood. No hostess tonight just luggage. I added the duffle and my pack to one side of the pile hoping later additions wouldn't bury them. Digging through a pile of luggage to reclaim mine didn't seem appealing.

Ron and Carl were having an interesting discussion about subsistence roe (salmon eggs) sales and the problems with the emergency regulation the governor had written making it legal. Some people instead of just catching what they needed for the winter were continuing to catch fall chums. Dumping the dead males and females after they striped of eggs. Then they would sell the bucket of eggs. Ron and Carl were in town for a meeting with people representing subsistence fishers, the Feds, Governor's office and such. I just sat quietly, sipping beer and soaking it all end. *This could be me someday.*

After Carl's round Ron bought a round. I was a little concerned about my turn, I would look funny paying with the all the quarters I had bought with my last ten so I could make phone calls. The beer on the plane and the two in the bar also had me concerned about making it down the Sharp's stairway without falling. Not drinking all summer had made me a lightweight. Luckily as my turn came Ron stood up and said "Carl do you want me to drop you at the hotel?"

"No, think I'll stay and see if that moo-moo comes off." Our waitress, nice enough woman, good at her job but way too old for me, was wearing a flowing moo-moo.

"OK, let's go Kim." I rose obediently.

I hadn't spoken since sitting down. The roe sales had started as pollical favor by Governor Egan for Hubert Humphrey, Senator from Minnesota, who I only remembered as a failed presidential candidate. "Ron why does a Senator from Minnesota want there to be subsistence roe sales in Alaska?"

"The guys who want to buy and sell roe are from Minnesota. Probably big campaign donors or something." Ron guessed.

Interesting, subsistence fishers don't use the eggs, so why not add to their income. Most are poor. Then greedy ones have to spoil it for the fish and reasonable people. Money is the root of all evil. Who said that? Bible I think.

Ron dropped me at the Sharp's and I snuck into the sleeping house and to the guest room in the basement I had used for a month the summer before. The next morning after a wonderful breakfast, if you don't count Betsy telling me my beard looked terrible. Bert kindly dropped me off at Fish& Game on his way to work. I came through the front door lugging all my gear which now included my shotgun which I stored at the Sharp's. Asking for the Commercial Fish office, I was directed through a door into a hallway that was partially blocked by a desk covered with fish tickets and all the other familiar gear of the fish ticket editor's trade. There were people with coffee mugs, overflowing into the hallway from the office opposite the editor's desk. I dumped my stuff next to the desk and waited for an opening in the conversation.

"Hi I'm Kim Francisco. I was supposed to report to Fred Anderson."

"Opps, time for work." One of the speakers said and the group broke-up and left. The fellow sitting at the desk in the office, not much older than me, called me in, extending his hand. "Hi.

I'm Fred Anderson, Geiger's assistant for the upper Yukon. Have a seat. Help yourself to the coffee." I emptied the Mr. Coffee pot into an unused mug and had a seat after turning the machine off.

"There's been a change in plans, of course. The subsistence crew hasn't made it back yet, there flying to upriver villages doing surveys. Our joint tagging crew with Sportfish, in Rampart, is short person because he returned to college so you get to go tag chum salmon and sheefish for a few days. That all right." Fred explained.

"Sure, I've never tagged fish but I'm willing to learn. Never seen a sheefish." I said, eagerly looking forward to some biology like you see on TV.

"Good. Sportfish is at the other end of the building. Go tell Ken Alt you're here to join the tagging crew. I've got to answer the damn phone, which had been ringing for a while, and get ready for that fucking meeting." I assumed the meeting was the one Ron and Carl were in town for, Fred seemed really busy so I headed across the building looking for Sportfish.

Oddly, given my years in Fairbanks I had only been past reception in the Fish& Game office once before to interview for a job with the moose research biologist John Cody the year before.

His office was next door to Fred's, I hadn't seen the other side of the building.

I walked through reception and into a "new" side of the office. A sea of desks surrounded by offices that monopolized most of the windows. As I approached the area with the Sportfish Division's sign hanging from the ceiling there was another office overflowing with people discussing something. Otherwise the area looked deserted except for a beautiful, small, delicate, blond behind a centrally located desk under the Sportfish sign. She was busy with a mountain of paperwork. I approached her tentatively waiting for her to lift her head from her task. She probably felt my presence because she look-up and asked "Can I help you?".

"I hope so. I'm Kim Francisco, with Commercial Fisheries Division, I'm supposed to report to Ken Alt to be part of the joint tagging team."

"Ken, Mr. Alt's office is there, where the morning staff meeting is happening." She pointed to the office of conversing people. She got up, great figure, perfect legs, saying "Come with me." Without any warning or ceremony, she moved to the edge of the crowd overflowing from the office and said "Ken there is someone here to see you?" She turned and walked back to her desk. Someone said "Eunice is sending us back to work." The group broke-up rather quickly going by me on both sides. There were two desks left in the office one with a blond fellow, a little older than me and the other a dark-haired fellow who was thirty something. A tall, rough looking fellow had stayed seated in one of the guest chairs when the group broke up.

"Hi Mr. Alt, I'm Kim Francisco with Commercial Fish, I'm suppose too help with a tagging project." I said to the blond who was looking at me.

The blond one said, "Hi but I'm Steve Tack this is Ken." He nodded his head towards the older dark-haired fellow who was rising to his feet. "Good morning Kim. I'm Ken." We shook hands while he continued. "The tagging project is mine. This guy is Terry Bendock, he's the crew leader in Rampart. Your flight leaves at 9:30. Terry, why don't you show Kim which truck to put his gear in. You are ready to go?" Ken asked?

"Yes, it's all at Comm. Fish." I said.

"Good. Terry, you guys load-up, I'll be out in a few minutes to drive you to the airport." Ken finished his instructions.

Terry stood, *wow he's a long way up there.* I put my hand out "Nice to meet you Terry."

We shook firmly he said "Back at Ya. The truck is around back." "OK, I'll go grab my stuff from the front door." I said.

"Can you get it or do you need some help?" Terry offered.

"Nope, I got it." I said.

I retraced my steps and grabbed my gear. Terry was standing at the back of the lobby at the back doors. He held the doors for my exit. "You ever done this before?" He asked.

"No, I've been editing fish tickets in Emmonak all summer. Looking forward to a change." I answered.

"Emmonak, where's that?" Terry asked.

"The mouth of the Yukon River. It's not the end of the world but you can see it from there."

Laughing, he asked "You didn't like it?"

"Sorry if I gave the wrong idea. No, I loved it. But I'm looking forward to this, actually working with live fish. I'm still having dreams about taking A-W-L samples." I said tossing my gear into a pickup Terry patted with his hand.

"Good, you won't have to learn that part. Except, the sheefish, we take total length not that weird mid-eye to fork stuff you Commfish guys do.

Sheefish are amazing, they reproduce successfully even though there are no Hefish!"

Laughing, I said "good one."

At the airport we boarded a Cessna 207, with two other passengers. The pilot had us all seated in the four seats right behind his. Terry asked for and got the right seat next to the pilot. He explained he was leaning to fly. The rest of the plane was pretty well filled with cargo, boxes of can goods, fresh produce, even a couple cases of milk with some mail bags on top. The luggage joined the cargo and the line boy and pilot threw a black net over the whole stack, securing it and the cargo to the floor with clips that fastened into the seat rails.

I loved the flight over the boreal forest and its many ponds and lakes. In spite of my worries about missing Marie on all my phone calls. The tops of the Steese Mountains were alpine tundra that had already turned into a miniature display of fall colors. *What a job and I get paid to do it.*

Rampart, our destination, was the first stop. We landed on a gravel runway at one end of the village which was perched over the river and under the hills, that would have been mountains back home in Iowa. It was beautiful.

The cargo/flight agent at Rampart was an elderly man, who looked none to fit. He quickly took advantage of our willing hands and directed Terry and I in how to off-load the cargo on to a pickup that appeared to be in worst shape than him and just as old. The license plates were missing. He took off in a cloud of blue smoke when loaded.

"Shit, thought he'd at least give us a ride for our help." Terry said.

"Yeah, not exactly a friendly bastard. He does fog for bugs wherever he goes." I noted.

Mean time the mosquitos had discovered us so we were busy finding the Deet in our gear and dousing ourselves. We both had the same stuff in green plastic bottles from the Army Surplus store on Ft Wainwright. It was stronger than anything available at drug stores, it was 100% Deet.

"You know this stuff isn't safe for babies. Wonder why it's safe for adults?" I asked.

"Shit works. It's either die of cancer when your seventy from using it or die of blood loss now." Terry explained.

We put on our packs and headed down the road. Terry pointing out the houses along the way. Most were picturesque log cabins built from the surrounding forest. There was one frame house with clapboard siding that had seen better days. It was one of the oldest in the village, Terry had been told it once had been a Hudson Bay's trading post, back when England and the US were determining the border. After that was settled, Rampart was in Alaska, it became a Northern Commercial post. Now it was a Mom and Pop store stocked with treats and necessities. We walked the length of the village and arrived at another white frame house with various log outbuildings, caches and a couple of nylon tents in the front yard.

"Here we are." Terry announced. "This is Peter Oates house. We're chartering his fishwheel for the tagging project. I'm in that red tent but the green one is empty so help yourself.

The outhouse is out back. Open air kitchen there." There was a nylon tarp on five poles, each corner and center. An old wooden table, most recently white, was under the tarp with a portable propane stove on top, the twenty-five gallon tank underneath.

Home sweet home. Have to recommend to Geiger the propane setup, nicer than the white gas. Whoever was here last left the tent clean. Need to unroll the Thermorest so it inflates.

Terry had walked over while I shook-out the Thermorest. "Hey, how does that thing work?

I've seen em in the catalogs but didn't know anyone who used one."

"I've had it about two years now. Real happy with it. Doesn't seem thick enough but it is, does a really good job of cushioning from the ground. Haven't sprung any leaks yet. You just shake it out and it self-inflates."

"Good to know. Peter doesn't seem to be around. When you're done there, we will go out to the wheel and tag some salmon. I've been gone since yesterday. We usually empty the live box three times a day. Poor sheefish will probably be dead." Terry said.

"Let me change into my rubber boots and rain gear. Why will the sheefish be dead?" I asked.

"They're kind of delicate. This has been a long stretch without a check so the chums will have beaten the shees to death by now."

"That's too bad. Ready, let's go." I said.

"Got your raingear on, guess this isn't your first rodeo." Terry said.

Nice not to be a complete newbie. Figured the boat ride would be wet and sampling fish is always wet.

The riverbank was a short walk, a good thing since we were carrying a gas can, a large landing net and assorted gear. A large aluminum, rectangular shaped boat, probably twenty feet long with a sixty-five-horse outboard was tied to the bank. The boat was flat bottomed, their variously known as John boats or riverboats. Terry stepped in, hooked up the gas hose, and started the engine with smooth practiced motions. I untied and pushed off, jumping in as I pushed. I managed to do it smoothly enough that I looked experienced. Terry was standing, guiding the outboard with a tiller extension that allowed a standing position.

Remember Dad's favorite command "Trim up the boat".

Terry was standing in the starboard rear stern of the boat. I took a seat on the port forward seat to put the boat on an even keel. We headed up stream with the beautiful rocky cliffs rising on each side ahead of us. The Ramparts that gave the village its name. The fish wheel was just ahead of us. Mr. Oates had built it from local trees, it was much larger than the ones I had seen in the Tanana River. The baskets were probably twenty feet in length. Positioned opposite each other, they were probably eight feet wide covered in about two-inch mesh tared net twine. The main beams of the basket had once been small spruce trees and were gracefully curved at the top by the shorter braces that pulled the tops back towards the trunks. At a ninety-degree angle to the baskets were two shorter paddles extending from the same axle. These were pushed by the current, giving the baskets their power to dip into and then sweep upwards and out of the river. As the basket rose any passing fish caught were lifted on the netting, pulled by gravity down to the hub of the wheel. The bottom of the basket were chutes made of rough planks, worn smooth by fish sliding across them. The chutes were slanted so gravity continued sliding the fish down the chute into a box mounted on the outboard float of the wheel. The Oates' wheel's floats were four spruce logs about twenty feet long and at least a foot in diameter. Unlike a normal commercial/subsistence fish-wheel, most were both, the sportfish staff had replaced the dead box on the float with a live box set in the water. This also required and extension on the chute to carry the fish over the float. They then splashed down in a rectangular box made of a 2x4 frame covered in a small mesh nylon knotless netting.

A plywood front piece broke the current to save the fish from exhausting themselves swimming constantly upstream.

I didn't see all this detail until after I jumped out onto the float. I tied up while Terry set out the measuring board on the boat's front seat. He then opened a small tackle box that we had carried down to the boat and set out the Floy Tag gun and some strips of tags to load the gun. On the other side of the measuring board he lay out a bundle of six-inch long heavy gauge needles held by a rubber band. These would be inserted through center holes in plastic fluorescent orange disks about ¾" in diameter, known as Peterson Disks. Which were waiting, in numerical order on a single needle. Alongside these there were a plastic bag filled with blank disks, a pair of side cutters and clipboards with data sheets. One for salmon, one for sheefish.

There's always a clipboard or it isn't science.

"Get out of your coat. We get warm" Terry recommended as he tossed his float-coat into the back of the boat. I followed his lead, getting out of the float-coat revealing my Helly Hanson overalls.

"Hey, those will be perfect for this job. Keep the slime off but still let enough air in to keep cool. Wearing a full set of rain-gear gets hot some days. Helly Hanson is the best." Terry said.

"Yeah, these worked great A-W-L sampling in Emmonak. Still have some fish scales on them. Can't seem to wash those buggers off. The sales clerk in Anchorage didn't steer me wrong." I said.

"Here's the landing net. Take a sweep through the box and see what you get." Terry instructed.

"This will be fun!" I said taking the net.

"The first five or ten times but after a few hundred its work." Terry warned.

Standing over the live-box I replied "Yeah, all sampling is the same. Death by repetition." I pushed the net in at the back of the box. The net frame had been bent from its original oval to a rectangle that just fit between the sides of the box that was boiling with fish. I pushing it down in to the bottom, I felt it hit several objects. When it hit bottom, I swung it forward and about fell off the float when the unexpected weight of a net full of fighting salmon was too much for me. Chum salmon spilled into the box and onto the float from the overflowing net. The ones that landed on the float quickly flipped themselves into the river. Except one wrong-way Corrigan who managed to drop off the other side back into the wheel as it was rising out of the river.

"Just one at a time please." Terry said laughing.

I tipped the net forward into the box letting all but one of the remaining salmon return to the box, before swinging the net and fish over to Terry in the boat.

"Hop in and write down the data." Terry said.

I climbed back into the boat, picked up the clipboard with the familiar A-W-L sheet on it.

"Hey, Write-In-the-Rain paper, that's nice, some of ours got a little rough after getting wet."

"Yeah, Eunice got a bunch of Write-In the Rain that you just load in the Xerox machine and print out your forms. Salmon go into the measuring board like your use too." Terry filled me in.

"No, we had a meterstick with an adjustable slide and pointer. Our fish were dead so lied there compliantly. This V-shaped box with a meterstick screwed into one side is pretty slick.

Kind a like a squeeze chute for cattle. I like your board." I said.

I recorded the sex and length he called out.

"Take a disk, number 2667, record that in comments. Slide it onto a needle, be sure the number is on the outside. Then just behind the dorsal fin about an inch down you slide the needle through the back." Terry slide the needle through keeping the salmon firmly pinned in the V with his free hand. The fish struggled big time but settled down after the needle was in. "Who ever said fish don't feel pain, never tagged them with a Peterson disk." I commented.

"Not sure if its pain exactly, not the way we feel it, but they sure feel it. Take a blank disk out of the bag, thread it on the needle. Use the needle nosed pliers to bend and twist the needle tight. Like this." Terry twisted the needle around the nose of the pliers. "Cut off the extra with the side cutters. You're done." Terry picked the struggling salmon out of the box and gave it a gentle toss over the side of the boat into the river. "Just stay on this side of the border, you slimy bastard." Ready for another."

"Coming right up." I repeated the dipping process.

"That last guy I had thought getting in and out of the boat was too much work." Terry commented.

"If I get tired I'll let you know." I said.

Things went faster, the tags were in order so I just filled in the next number while I had free moments. A-W-L was old hat. I grabbed the blank disks, handing them to Terry as needed.

The changes in the chums was interesting. They had begun getting their spawning colors so none would have been graded number one. I expected from what the Japanese buyers had shown me they would have all been number threes. Sexing by exterior appearance was much simpler, the males were developing their strong hooked jaws and teeth for fighting. The females didn't have the change in their faces but were much more obviously gravid with round distended bellies.

After several chums, I came up with a new fish. About the same length as the chums, about five hundred millimeters, but not nearly as deep or robust. *Wow, my mind has changed, fish are millimeters long not inches. Still think in English units for everything else. Twenty-five mills are an inch so guess that thing is 20 inches.*

"Hey, think I've got my first sheefish. It doesn't look so good." I said stepping into the boat.

"Yep, the chums have beat her badly. Better rush this. Should be a data sheet under your salmon sheets." Terry reminded me..

"Got it."

"Five hundred and seventeen. Female. Tag number 2753." He inserted the Floy Tag gun's needle behind the dorsal fin then pulled the trigger. One of the stringy tags came off the strip into the fish. The inserted part of a Floy tag is a small but strong piece of plastic string that ends in a T. The head of the T is folded against the string going in by the gun's hollow needle but after it leaves the needle it opens up to be at ninety degrees to the string, anchoring the tag to the fish. The external part of the tag has a thicker bright orange casing with the tag number. Terry quickly injected the tag then gently leaned over the edge of the boat holding her in the current.

"Hope she comes around." He said.

"What happens if resuscitation doesn't work?" I asked.

"You get to cross out the data line and have your first sheefish supper. There she goes."

He said as the sheefish swam out of his hands. "Hope she makes it."

"Yeah, looks like it's tough sharing a box with the chums." I said.

"Sure is. You're probably going to find more, dead or nearly dead ones on the bottom.

Better fill the washtub." Terry pulled a large wash tub from amidships. The tackle box and other loose gear had been in it coming over so I thought it was just a storage container. He picked up a bucket filling it expertly over the side.

Until you try it, you might think you just stick a bucket in a river to fill it. Usually, depending of speed of water and boat, it will probably bounce off and you won't get much. But if you swing the bucket upstream, matching the speed of the current as you come down, it will slip right into the water and you can stand with a full bucket. Technique is different if you're in a high-sided boat or on a bridge. He filled the tub with several buckets. He poured the water from the bucket held almost at shoulder height so the long fall and splash would thoroughly aerate it.

"If you've thinned out the chums enough to get to the bottom of the box, try to take a pass and see if you can get any shees off the bottom. We'll put em in the tub to see if they recover enough to tag." Terry said.

"OK" I went back to work with the net but had to remove several more chums before I could make a pass on the bottom. Once I had thinned the chums enough, they could swim above the net, I was able to make a scoop along the bottom. Came up with a net-full of sad looking sheefish. The net was so heavy I had to choke up on the handle so I could grab the outer rim with my left to lift it. I quickly stepped off the float into the boat, almost going into the river since my sea legs weren't use to a net load of fish. But the sheefish made it to the tub. I stayed out of the river. I got a few more healthier ones with my next scoop. Also, an unwanted chum that I was able to let "escape" back into the box. Terry was adding a bucket of fresh water to the tub to boost the oxygen. My third try took us back to chum tagging. Turned out there was a sheefish I had missed. The biggest one over six hundred millimeters. She was a dandy, either had held her own because of her size or more likely was just recently caught. We finished the chums then checked our recovery tank. Terry had been regularly adding water to keep the oxygen level up as we worked the chums. All but two had perked up and were swimming. Being a wellpracticed team now, we quickly measured and tagged the swimmers. When gently held in the water after tagging most soon swam off. One had still been lethargic in the tank. Tagging didn't improve him much. Terry was bent over the side a long time with him. He did finally make a couple of strong kicks and swam out of Terry's hands. That burst of energy evidently exhausted him, he was still near enough the surface of the muddy river that we could see him turn and let the current take him downstream.

"Hope he makes it." I said.

"Yeah, probably not. The chums probably beat him to badly and he'll die of internal injuries. Just left the box too long. Won't happen now that we're both here." We were talking as we cleaned up and put things away for the trip back.

"Is the sheefish study part of the chum salmon international study?" I asked.

"No, Ken's been working on them for a while. Piggybacking with the chum study just provided an extra funding source and a way to stretch the tagging season. It was good for Comm. Fish since Ken runs it. Fred doesn't really have time and I guess the research guys in Anchorage don't either." Terry explained.

I started untying the boat amidships by the time I got to the bowline, Terry had untied the stern and started the engine. As soon as the boat was on step, Terry folded his tall body down so he could reach the drain plug in the transom while still driving and pulled it out. The extra water from the overflowing recovery tank and from the fish being tagged soon drained out. Terry replaced the plug.

Back at Peter Oats, I volunteered to fillet the sheefish. One skill I had developed in childhood. My Dad had taught me his technique, which I modified with information from my Fishing Merit Badge book. Later, when my family was on our annual fishing trip in Ontario. I was slowly cleaning our day's catch in the fishing camp's fish house. A couple of guides came in with their client's catch. They zipped through them and left with a parting shots about the kid who didn't know what he was doing. A Native American guide came in with his client's fish and as his knife flashed through them almost under my nose from his side of the table, I was getting a little frightened. In spite of Native American history being a hobby and my feeling that they hadn't gotten a fair shake, to many cowboy vs Indians TV shows and movies left a little fear, when I was alone with a knife wielding Indian. He finished a couple of fish and put up a fresh one looked over at me and smiled as I put a fresh fish on the table.

"Mind I show you quicker way to fillet?" He asked.

"Yeah, that would be nice." I said in a choked whisper.

He walked around to my side with his knife in his hand. I was thinking of picking up mine but he beat me to it. He flexed it against the table then tested the edge on his thumb.

"Good knife, not sharp enough." He took a small sharpening stone from his pocket and began stroking the knife on it. He bent down so the knife and stone were in front of my eyes.

"Like this, like shaving the stone." My fear of an unknown disappearing as this kind thoughtful man shared his knowledge. I watched carefully, knife sharping was a skill I had long tried to develop. My new teacher handed me the knife and stone and I tried.

"No, angle wrong. I show you." He said stepping behind me he surrounded me with his arms and took my hands adjusting my grip on the stone then guiding my strokes. Then he tested it again on his thumb drawing blood. "Sharp now. Ok, slice behind gills till you hit spine. There feel spine?" My hands still in his, guided my knife hand through the walleye till it stopped.

"Yes." I answered.

"Ok, turn knife and draw down spine, feel for ribs. There feel ribs?" He asked guiding my hand.

"Yes." I said.

"Ok, lift handle so front blade stays on spine and back on top of ribs. Pull down fish. Good, STOP." I about jumped out of my skin.

We were about ½ an inch from the tail.

"This hinge, you want. OK, flip filet over, like this." The method I knew you didn't leave a hinge, you just took the whole fillet off. Then using knife and/or pliers you loosened a piece of skin at the tail and then pulled as much as you could off the fillet. The skin usually broke repeatedly and you continued the struggle. My new teacher took my hand as I hesitated and pushed it away from the fish. Now the fillet was on the table skin side down but still attached to the carcass by the bent hinge of flesh and skin.

"Put knife in hinge, don't cut skin. Turn so blade between skin and meat. Don't cut hinge." He guided my hand again. "OK, use other had grab fish, slide knife between skin and meat. Like this." The knife seemed to glide along between the skin and meat. Zip, there was a skinned fillet in seconds, with pliers it usually took five to ten minutes.

"Wow, that's great. I should have figured that out watching you guys. Thank you very much." He stepped away. "Show me. Do other side" *Teachers always give a test.*

I obeyed. I never did completely master sharpening knifes and rarely got the rib removal in one slice right. But it improved my fish cleaning and I got to teach it to my father. Who went on to teach others the technique in Iowa and elsewhere. He always said "We learned it from an Indian guide in Canada." Connecting it to an Indian guide somehow gave it greater authority. Always struck me odd that these same people said terrible things about Native Americans. Dad's "we" rankled a bit too. He learned it from me.

Terry cooked while I was washing up. The sheefish was delicious, along with baked beans.

We tried something new Terry had found at the store in Fairbanks during his brief trip to town. Dehydrated ice cream. It was surprisingly good. Best of all you could sneak it past the bean counters in Juneau as dehydrated food. Ice cream was on the forbidden list.

Peter Oates joined us for supper. He had towed in a small log raft of the trees he had cut.

He beached his boat and raft in front of his house next to our boat.

"Peter join us for supper. There's plenty." Terry greeted him as he came up the bank.

"Won't logs be a little green for burning this winter." Terry asked when Peter sat down with a full plate.

"Nah, only cut dead trees. Already dry." Peter answered.

Swallowing my mouthful of sheefish, I asked "I don't see a snow-go. How do you run your trapline?" His traps were hanging out under his elevated cache to keep human scents off them so I knew he was a trapper.

"Dem five dogs." He nodded towards the back of the house, where five sled dogs were chained to their houses. "Snowgo don't start, forty below, you kick and kick it, still won't start.

Dogs they always start."

"But couldn't you make more money covering more area?" Terry asked.

"Nah, just spend more money on snowgo and gas. Dogs eat salmon I catch and dry. I do better than guys with snowgo." Peter answered.

Basic economics, lower cost equals more profit.

"What about trail sets? Don't dogs get in traps?" I asked thinking of the trail sets Bert and I used.

"Not my dogs. I say whoa, they whoa. Race dogs just run. No good." Peter said.

"Why don't you have log house?" I asked, changing the subject.

"Log cabins on trapline. This house grandfather's. He trader here in Rampart.

Grandmother wanted real house. He built this for her." Peter explained.

Wow, this is an old house. Still in pretty good shape considering Peter's lack of care.

His grandfather and father must have spent more time on the house.

"Any salmon tomorrow?" Peter asked.

"Kim's pretty good help and the run seems to be getting stronger so we should get our quota tagged and have fish for you, tomorrow or next day" Terry answered.

"Good, need dry more." Peter got up and walked up to the house. He looked tired but full.

"I really admire that guy. He still lives without hardly any money. But watching him and how hard he has to work to live a subsistence life sure ruined the idea of running away and living off the land for me." Terry said.

"Yeah, those cabin folks on campus sure discover living off the land isn't all it's cracked up to be. They really are just saving money on cheap rent by going without plumbing and central heat. Wonder if that really has a lower environmental impact on the world like they claim. I mean, all the trees cut for cabins and fire-wood and I'm not sure wood smoke is any better for the atmosphere than oil heat, certainly worse than propane."

"That's for sure. Trouble with figuring something like that out, is there are so many things you have to account for. If you use a snow-machine or pick-up, hell even an outboard like Peter to get wood. You burn gas. Then there's chainsaw gas and oil. Manufacturing all that stuff has impacts. If you go really low impact with handsaws and axes you'll soon learn to go with less heat. Damn chainsaw broke last winter and I tried to cut my wood with a handsaw. Takes fucking forever to cut a night's wood." Terry filled in.

Oops, didn't know he was a cabin dweller. Hope I didn't offend. "You got that right. You don't realize how much living takes till you reduce it to basics. You cooked. My turn for dishes."

❦

Next morning's radio check changed everything again.

"KE6628 Rampart this is KE6628 Fairbanks." Peter let us keep the radio on his front porch.

That way it stayed dry and could be plugged in.

This radio routine is starting to get old.

"This is KE6628 Rampart, go ahead." Terry answered.

"Be sure to meet tomorrow's mail plane. Kim's, replacement will be on board. Kim, you return to Fairbanks. We're sending you to Tanana. Got that. Over."

"Fairbanks this is Rampart. Got it. Groceries are getting a little low. Do you want a list?

Over"

Guess Terry uses better radio procedure in case the FCC in Fairbanks is listening or is it working on his pilot's license?

"Rampart this is Fairbanks back. We already have groceries so we don't need a list.

They'll be on the plane. Over."

Terry looked at me. "Anything else?" he asked.

"Nah. Wonder what the guy I'm meeting in Tanana is like?"

Fairbanks this is Rampart back. Rampart clear."

"Finally get a good hand and they're going to switch you out. Wonder what kind help the new guy there sending will be? They should just send him on the subsistence survey." Terry complained.

"Thanks. Hope you get another good hand. I sort of wish I could stay. This is a good job but doing the trip down the Yukon is something

I'm looking forward too. Plus, I had a little survey experience in Emmo. Should I ask if you could go along with me?" I said.

"Temping, but no, then Ken would have to train to new guys. I'd like making that trip. I'm just getting tired of training new guys. There are a surprising number of people who think you don't have to work when you work for the fucking state." Terry said.

We continued our profane if not profound conversation about lazy help as we loaded the boat for the morning wheel check. When we arrived, a mink scampered down the float from the live box carrying a cisco in his mouth.

"Lazy or smart, little shit. Nothing like catching fish that are already caught." Terry greeted the mink. I tied up the boat and fished the net out.

"An interesting philosophical conundrum." I commented.

"Fuck yourself. To early for your smart mouth." Replied Terry.

"Nice to know I'll be missed. "The box is filled to overflowing, the poor sheefish." My words became prophetic as a chum slid down the chute to drop in the box. In the resulting melee of splashing fish trying to find room to swim, two squirmed out. One right over the side, the other got caught in the gap between the float logs and began struggling its way down the float to me. I took a couple of steps, reached down and picked him up firmly.

"You ready for a customer?" I asked.

"Nah, still getting organized over here."

"Your lucky day, have a good time spawning." I pitched my squirming captive into the river. My Fishing merit badge booklet recommended wetting your hands before handling a fish you're going to release. The idea being it protected the fishes' protective slimy barrier. Which made sense. On paper. What field biologists had learned and Terry taught me, was it was a lot harder to hold on to a squirming fish with wet hands which resulted in more injuries. Some studies were done to test different methods of handling. Taking a firm grip with dry hands or gloves, being careful to support as much as the fishes' weight as possible turned out to have the best long-term survival. They also learned that just because a fish swims away doesn't mean it will live. A couple of traditional methods of fish handling like jawing, lifting by the lower jaw and tailing, lifting by the tail, were found to result in high mortality days or months after handling the fish.

Their able to swim away but with a broken or sprained jaw or back, which made making a living as a fish pretty tough.

With the box so full, I was able to dip fish to tag from the boat. Which speeded up the process. Also saved a lot of work stepping in and out. Before adopting this technique, I had tried to make a deep scoop to rescue sheefish off the bottom. The resulting chaos sent a few more chums on their way without a tag to show their friends.

After the first dozen or so we both stood for a much-needed stretch. Terry freshened his chew, offering me a pinch out of his snuff.

"Nope, I'll stick to my pipe."

"Hey, this is hands free, you can do it while you work."

"Yeah, about the grossest thing I ever heard was from my neighbor in the dorm Tim Dooley. He finally got a date and it turned into a whole floor production but mostly mine to get him ready. After he showered, shaved, for the first time in who knows how long. He needed clean underwear, which he didn't have so I loaned him a pair of mine. Clean pants and shirt, from two other guys. Fresh condom, from one of the other guys. Optimistic for a first date. Twenty bucks, mine. He had his own snoose, Copenhagen, like yours. Off he went. Two A.M. he wakes me up. "Kim, I'm in love. When we were French kissing we traded snoose. She uses some sissy mint flavored crap, going to have to get her to change. I'm in fucking heaven. What a girl. You want your underwear back?"

I said "You keep the boxers but I want back the twenty." Man, can you imagine trading snoose."

"Don't think I'd want to date a girl who chewed. Guess that makes me a male chauvinist pig." "Terry said thoughtfully.

"Or just smart. What does it say about a girl who dates a chewer?" I said. "Fuck you."

"Please somebody. *The traditional Lathrop Hall reply.* I better start handing fish down.

Think were catching them faster than tagging them."

"Yeah the run is really going."

Later we had a whooper bull chum. He was too big for the measuring cradle so I was pinning him to the seat while Terry measured him with a tape measure, then began tagging him. Usually when you slid the pin in the fish just gave a body wide quiver. Every now and again we hit a tender spot and the fish bucked and slapped for all it was worth. They are surprisingly strong. Unluckily Terry hit a tender spot on this big one who was thirty something pounds of pure muscle and slime. My left hand went flying and my left cheek was smashed and slimed by his head as he flew off the seat and onto the boat deck. Terry grabbed for him as he scooted across the deck. I stepped over the seat reaching down to grab him. Our timing was perfect Terry and I slammed our heads together.

"Shit!" we said in unison.

"Damn fucking fish, we should kill him for Peter." I said as the fish struggled across the deck.

"Nope, we signed on to face adversity. Get him. We'll tag that sucker and then clean up this mess he made out of the tackle box." Our subject had managed to spill and spread the contents of the tackle box, with all the tagging gear, over the deck. I pinned him in a corner between the deck and rear seat, picked him up and held him in a bow-shape, pulling the head towards the tail. He froze. Terry quickly pinned the tag to him.

"Let him go." Terry said.

I threw the freshly tagged fish over the side. "There, you fucker, may you swim into the next fishwheel or a bear make you lunch."

"That last paralyzing hold was pretty slick. You just invent that?" Terry asked.

"Nah, our struggle reminded me of Geiger telling about using it on a king tagging project. Geiger said everyone else would come out of the tagging sessions covered in slime and beat to pulps. This Yup'ik guy who used the bow trick always looked like he just stepped out of a shower. So, they all started using it. It worked!" I explained.

"I haven't spoken to Geiger much, he never said much, he's not that way all the time huh?" Terry asked.

"Not always, if you find something he's interested in. I'm told by Reardon, the guy I'm replacing on subsistence survey, that his Dad was an area biologist back when Geiger started. Guess he was a wild guy but got in some trouble and calmed way down. Regnart told me Geiger is real friendly once he gets to know you. But he didn't have much to say this summer. Unless its baseball. The villagers call him stone face."

Laughing Terry said "I can see that."

We went back to work tagging. Three sheefish were tagged, they were running stronger too. But we had four dead, one for supper and three for Peter's drying rack. We hadn't quite finished with the fish when we hit the magic number, sixty. Terry stretched his back, it had been a long session and we had a plane to meet.

"We made the daily goal. First time for that. Ken says the Canadians are paying us by the tag and their biometrician said not more than sixty a day."

"Those three sheefish we tagged were in good shape. To bad about the others. Is there a goal on them?"

"Nope, supposed to tag till the tags run out. If Ken's guess is right, these aren't fully anadromous, they just drop down into the lower river for the winter not the ocean. But that's what we're tagging them for is to find out." Terry informed me.

"Why does he think that?" I asked.

"Because their much smaller at maturity than the ones up on the Kobuk River, which do go all the way to Kotzebue Sound or further. Those get up to fifty pounds." Terry answered.

"Wow, king salmon size." I exclaimed.

"Yeah, the guides up there sell fishing trips for the tarpon of the north." Terry said.

"Love to try that someday. Hey what do we do with the rest of these salmon in the box?"

"Club 'em so Peter will have some dog food." Terry said.

I fished out the remaining chums and dumped them into the boat. As I stepped back into the struggling mess Terry handed me a two-foot length of 2x4 that had all its square edges rounded off and ended in a nice round handle that fit a hand perfectly. It had a short loop of leather shoelace for hanging and wrapping around the wrist so it couldn't fall overboard. Craved and colored into the business end was the name FISH KILLER. I proceeded to whack chum salmon heads till they all lay still. As long as I grabbed and pinned them with my left so I had a clear shot at the sweet spot on top of the head between the gills and eyes it only took one stroke. The first few felt like sweet revenge for all the gill cover cuts, slaps in the face and other indignities their brethren had inflicted during the recent days of tagging. My blood lust was quickly satisfied and I comforted myself with the fact that sudden death by club stroke sure beat suffocating like so many thousands of their kind were doing in fish wheel boxes up and down the river. Job done I looked down at the twenty odd chums we had for Peter. *Nice haul. Those feelings of revenge were silly. Imagine what being jerked into a suffocating atmosphere by giants who manhandle you and stick a pin through your back must be like. Wonder if they think about it afterwards?*

"You know only once in my life have I taken back this many fish. A friend and I caught 110 bluegills with our flyrods at a pond. Catching them was great. After cleaning about ten, I was convinced never to be so greedy again." I told Terry.

"You're in luck today, Peter will be cleaning them all." He replied.

"We're not going to help?" I asked.

"Nope, he won't let us. The first guy I had helped and botched the job so bad Peter won't let anyone near the fish now. You have to catch the plane." Terry reminded me.

"I didn't get a chance in Emmo. I was helping Mrs. Mosses and her lovely daughter Irene by cutting wood. They wouldn't let me cut fish because it was women's work." "I take it they aren't liberated yet. Did you score with Irene?" Terry said.

"No, she wasn't that kind of girl. We did date for about a month and I thought it might be the real thing but she broke it off." I explained.

"To bad, but at least your safe from marriage." Terry said laughing.

"Probably not. I met Marie latter and we ended up living together. She's back in college in Seattle but when they lay me off I'm Seattle bound. Casting off forward." I said.

"Were loose asswards." Terry's play-on-words was drowned out by the outboard roaring to work.

We unloaded the fish. Loaded my gear. I washed out the boat with buckets of river water while Terry kept it running upriver just fast enough to drain the water out of the drain. With everything ship shape, we took the boat to the airport just in time.

I left, thinking about phoning Marie in Fairbanks. I didn't know it then but Terry and I would be partners again the next fall but not tagging salmon in Rampart.

SUBSISTENCE SURVEY

"Welcome to Tanana folks." The pilot announced as the twin Otter landed.

My luggage came off. Looked like the shotgun was intact. With Marie on my mind I had forgotten my concern for my Browning Featherweight shotgun that was strapped to my pack.

Now that it was bird season, I hopped to have time to shoot some fresh meat. Hadn't had a chance in Rampart. Even with the hard "airline" case, I worried the barrel would get bent, so I had taken it from the action. It was a two-gun case so there was room for the barrel on the inside along the spine of the case. Figured that was the hardest place to bend. *One of these days I'm going to get to fish or hunt. Thought that was the point of this career. Forget Marie. You had a cry. Now we just add her to all of our other bad experiences with women and swear off them, until the next one. How's the song go "tomorrow I'll probably love again". One of Linda's[48] records. Remember, we rewrote it one-day fishing in a canoe.*

Weren't catching anything so changed love to fish. Fit perfectly.

I shouldered my pack, picked up my shotgun case and walked out the door. *Wonder where this George character is at? Thought he'd meet the plane.* Once outside the airport gate there was a road that ran parallel to the runway in the direction of the river. *Now get your shit together, stupid.*

Trying not to think of Marie, had the complete opposite effect. Cheering up was coming hard. Instead I found myself running through love's failures. *Kim, we might have been a confusing couple. June, classic me, flirted for three years in high school homeroom, finally in frustration at graduation she came over and gave me my first real kiss, then asked "Why didn't you ever ask me out?" "I didn't think you'd go." Was my brilliant reply. She moved to Texas the next day. I should go to Austin and look for her if I'm traveling this fall. Never been to Texas. Yeah, June Grace, my god she was beautiful. Jackie, her sister, told me she sat home alone almost every night.*

---

[48] My sister.

145

Stupid, didn't realize Jackie was telling me to ask her out. Older and wiser now. Hah! That's it, Texas bound to find June.

These thoughts and plans finally drove the tears away. I was set to meet a new work partner. *Good thing he didn't meet the plane.* The gravel road ended in a trail through the grass and weeds at the end of the airport. The trail came out on the river bank too steep for beaching boats. I looked up stream, I could see a small collection of boats on a small "beach". I moseyed up towards the boats. The Wahoo stuck-out like a sore thumb among the collection of boats on the beach. Most were river boats, like I'd been using at Rampart.

There were also a couple of greyhounds, boats built and designed for the big Tanana River 150 race. It was 150 river miles, more or less, depending on how the channel shifted, from Fairbanks to Tanana. Every year there was a big race, airboats not allowed, but big expensive race boats were. They had souped-up auto engines that when running at full throttle you could hear for miles. There were lots of wrecks every year but hardly anywhere for spectators to watch. They had to go out on the river to find a spot to watch from. I'd gone to the start once in Fairbanks. Thrilling but not my idea of a pleasant boat trip. The Wahoo sat there looking kind of dumpy, gray hull and green cabin, I could still pick out some of my brush strokes in the paint. *Look a lot better if Geiger had taken Reardon's suggestion to go with state colors, blue and gold. O well, guess gray and green was cheap.* I stepped aboard and shrugged my pack off, simultaneously dropping it on deck while calling "Hey, anyone named George here."

A groggy voice replied from the cabin, "Who wants to know?"

"Kim Francisco, we're supposed to take the Wahoo back to Emmonak."

Lots of sounds from the cabin as George was getting his boots on and waking up from his nap. The little cabin door popped open and a baseball cap on top of a bent over body came out. They didn't call it a dog house because it was roomy.[49] I greeted George with an outthrust hand as he stood up. He was about 4 inches taller than me, six two or three and heavy set like me. Not lean and hard like Terry. Light colored hair, couldn't decide if it was red or blond, sticking out from under a Fish and Game baseball cap.

---

[49] The Wahoo's was known as a "Cordova Dog House" skiff.

Wonder where he got the cap? I'd like one of those. <u>Who can grip the hardest handshakes, huh?</u> **Lost that test.** "Have you made this run before?" I asked, sort of assuming he was a regular late season employee.

"Nope, you?" He answered.

Will he always be so taciturn? "No, my first time too. Did work in Emmo this summer and got the boat ready for the trip upstream. Helped Reardon and Allo with the survey in Alakanuk and Emmo."

"Don't know Allo, met Reardon at airport, handed me a briefcase and got on the plane. In a hurry." George said.

"Any surveys left to do in Tanana?" I asked.

"Don't know. Don't like paperwork. Checked the boat out. You need to pay marina for gas.

We need groceries. Then we can go." George summarized recent events.

You only napped today. "You know the job's not done till the paperwork is finished." I quoted a line I'd heard from past supervisors.

"Huh"

"When you take a shit or do anything else, paperwork." *Doesn't like my sense of humor, good thing he's not working with Reardon. This isn't starting well. Just keep trying.*

George continued a puzzled look.

"I jokes." I slipped into village English.

"What?"

"It was a joke, "I jokes", it's a favorite phrase of the Yup'iks." *Going to be long trip if I have to explain every joke.*

"Yup'iks?"

"The Eskimo tribe down at the mouth of the Yukon, where I worked last summer." *Seems to take everything literally, have to keep things to business until we get to know each other. Terry was easier.*

"Let's see what Reardon left for us." I sat down on one of the big rectangular gas tanks built into the boats bulwarks. Opened the brief case George handed me, it was stuffed full of folders and subsistence calendars, on top was a one paragraph note.

"Hi Cisco Each folder is a village. Checked off names of the people we interviewed. You guys need to do the unchecked ones. Found most people. Except Tanana Allo and I had to go back to register so we didn't get many. Good luck. Mike Reardon.

Paperclipped to the note was a worn and beaten operational plan for the subsistence survey. *Looks like he had it out in the rain. Sooner started sooner done.* "They only did about half of Tanana, they were in a hurry to register. We better get started if were going get out of here."

"OK, boat's ready." George said.

"Yeah, don't need the boat, this is a mare's shank job." I explained.

"Huh."

"Mare's shank, it's an expression, means walking. We have to find out where these people live," I held up the clip board with list of names for Tanana and empty survey forms, "then you ask if they have their subsistence calendar. Most people didn't keep it, but it's our foot in the door." *No question, must know that one, kinda glazed look.* "Then you just ask them the questions on the form and fill in the answers. First couple are hard but then you get the hang of it. You still with me?" I asked.

"No, I won't do that." George said.

"You won't do what?" It was my turn to be dense.

"Ask strangers questions." George said.

"That's the job, what did you think you'd be doing?" I asked.

"Taking a boat down the Yukon and winterizing it." George answered simply. Grinding my teeth. *Now what do I do. Geiger must have explained. Doesn't want to do his job. Pull rank?*

"Are you a Tech III?" George looked a little surprised at my question and shift of topic.

"Yes."

Shit can't pull rank. Maybe crew leader? Date of hire? "Geiger tell you who was crew leader?" I asked.

"No."

"He told me I was." I lied. "I'm to teach you how to do the surveys. I'll come along for the first ones but then we have to split-up." *That will soften the blow.*

"No. I won't do it." George said.

Now what. Shot your wad. Lead by example. "Fine, fuck you. I got to get started. I grabbed the clipboard and slammed the brief case close." *Fucking leather case, doesn't close with emphasis.* I stood-up, climbed out and marched down the street towards the center of town. *Damn fucker, expect's me to do this whole thing by myself.* **Call Geiger.** *Tanana has phones? Saw* *one at airport. Maybe trade for Terry.* My failure as a supervisor continued to fill my thoughts as I walked into town looking for the village office. *Must be something besides being a tattletale to do?* I stopped and asked a couple of people where the village office was, they didn't know. They also didn't know any of the people on my list. Seemed like forever but I'm sure it wasn't really long and someone directed to the city manager's office. *Should've asked for city office, stupid.*

"Hi I'm Kim Francisco, I'm here doing the salmon subsistence survey for Fish and Game. I was wondering if I could get some help on where people live." I asked the man sitting behind a desk.

"Hi, Tom Baker[50], City Manager, I gave that other guy a copy of the residence map?"

"He had to go back to college and I took over without talking to him. Let me see if the map is in the briefcase. I explained sitting down. *"Read all the instructions before taking this test. The last instruction is always don't take this test". Now I know why so many teachers pull that stunt. Here it is stupid. Damn getting angry screws you up every time!* "I'm sorry to have bothered you, here's the map. Didn't think to look for it, most villages don't have one." I tried to cover my tracks.

It's no bother and it's good for me to know who's wandering around town. In case anyone asks. Mr. Baker answered.

"Could I borrow your phone? It's a reverse charge call." I asked.

"Sure, help yourself." He pointed to and empty desk with a phone and sat back down at his own.

Calling home had made the procedure of reversing the charge familiar. Call the operator, give her the number, then give her your name, then listen as she calls and asks if the person will accept the charges from the person calling. This was my first time calling Geiger. *I miss the radio. Never thought I'd say that. Probably a lousy way to start a new assignment. Calling the boss with trouble.*

After the operator talked to two clerks a familiar voice said "Geiger"

"Hi this is Kim. I'm in Tanana starting to finish the subsistence survey but George refuses to interview anybody. Am I the crew leader?" Long silence.

---

[50] My memory isn't that good. Made this name up too.

"You're the crew leader for the survey, George is the crew leader for operating the boat." Geiger answered.

Doesn't want me to sink another old boat. "OK. But is he supposed to help on the survey?" I asked.

"Yes."

"What do I do if he doesn't?" I asked.

"Tell me at the end and it will go on his evaluation." Geiger replied.

"Err, but that doesn't help now." I said.

"You'll have to work it out. Bye." Click

Didn't even get to say goodbye. Obviously, my call was unwelcome. Tell George it will go on his evaluation. Then follow his lead on the boat. Maybe being good crew will encourage his being good crew?

I set out. *Surveyed houses were crossed out on map. Houses whose owner was on list of subsistence fishers were circled. Looked like they did the ones closest to the river. A walk will cool me off. Go for the furthest house. Work back.*

"Hi. I'm Kim Francisco from Fish and Game, I'm here to pick-up your subsistence calendar."

The plump Athabascan woman, about five feet tall gave me a puzzled look.

"It was a white calendar with fish drawings, they sent out in June so you could record the salmon you caught." I explained, her eyes opened wide with recognition.

"We left in fish camp." She said a little alarmed.

"That's OK." Relief on her face. "I have a short questionnaire. I can just ask you about your fishing success. Then we don't need the calendar."

Her face opened in a friendly welcome, "Would you like tea?"

"Yes, please." Mike and Allo had taught me it was important to always accept offers of food and drink. As a result, you were usually floating in tea and coffee, stuffed to the gills with baked goods by the end of the day. Over a cup of tea and fresh dinner rolls, I discovered how many kings and chums the family had put up for winter. That they fished with a fishwheel not a net.

There were eight people in the family: her husband's mother, napping, her husband and two boys, they were out setting-up moose camp, and three girls, who were at school but would be home soon.

That's how my afternoon and evening were spent going door to door asking for the subsistence calendars and snacking on what was offered. I quit at the first house that was preparing supper. Didn't want to disturb people's meals. By the time I arrived back at the Wahoo, I was stuffed and my eyeballs were floating in urine. I swear my eyes were yellow from accumulated urine. The Wahoo was sitting at an angle, stern downstream, so I used it for cover and drained my balder.

"Who's there?" Came George's voice.

"The bogeyman." I announced, I was going to have to learn to live with him so he would have to learn to live with me.

His head came out of the cabin door. A defensive look on his face. "O, it's you."

Zipping up I said "Yep, little old me. I called Geiger. I'm the crew leader for the subsistence survey. If you don't help it goes on your evaluation." He started to speak and I held up my hand palm out. "You are the crew leader for operating the boat. If I screw-up as boat crew it goes on my evaluation. I went ahead and started on the surveys. Lot of people out getting ready for moose hunting but I finished about half of what was left here in Tanana. I would like your help tomorrow but if you don't, you don't. I don't give a fuck about your evaluation."

"Did you pay for the gas at the gas dock?" George asked, reminding me of one of my crew duties.

"Nope. Forgot. I'll take care of it tomorrow morning." I said.

"I already ate." He said.

"That's OK, ladies on the survey stuffed me to the gills. Probably not a very balanced diet; bread, rolls, cake, cookies and some pilot bread and peanut butter, but I'm full. Mom's not here to check on me." I replied.

George had come right out and closed the door to keep the mosquitos out, who were getting fierce. "You going out again?"

"Naw, getting to late and I'm pooped. Tagged chums with Bendock before I left Rampart this morning. Flew here and spent rest of the day walking. Us fish ticket editors don't get a lot of exercise. Let's get in before "Cyrano De Bugs Are Back" carries us off." I said.

"Who?"

"Just get in out of the bugs. I'll explain."

We ducked into the cabin and began hunting down and killing the mosquitoes that had come in with us. Not real sure who was hunting who?

"Cyrano De Bugs Are Back" slap "is the king of" slap, whack "the mosquitoes on" smack, slap, "Damn it, that nail is sharp. Going to have to flatten it. On "Beanie and Ceil"." Wham, slap, slap. I explained between mosquito killings.

"Don't watch kid's shows." George said.

Didn't watch kids shows. Who didn't grow-up watching cartoons. ""Beanie and Ceil" was a prime-time cartoon for children and adults. My Dad never missed it. As Cyrano's name shows. If my Mom was here, she'd tell you kids are baby goats not young humans." I rambled as I hunted mosquitos.

"Cartoons are for kids. Why would that name show it wasn't? What about goats?"

George said.

"My mother was a stickler about English usage. Baby goats are called kids. Young humans are children or child. How old were you when you first read Cyrano De Bergerac? I explained.

"No idea what you're talking about?" George said.

"Cyrano De Bergerac is the title character in a play. I thought everyone had to study it in English. Even though it's French. About the only play I ever liked, since it has war, swords and muskets. Even if it was about Frenchies and romance, but I could identify with Cyrano who was too shy to talk to girls. The movie was not so great. Should we light a Pick?" I asked.

"No, I hate that stuff almost as much as English." George said.

Geez, this is going to be a long trip. How can he hate English, it's what we speak. I got out my current book out and settled into my bunk.

At breakfast things went well. Turned out I was more skilled with a Coleman stove than George so I put out the rather scary flare-up he had and relit the stove. He was a good cook so I ended up with the dishes. We didn't say much about anything except what we needed to fix breakfast and write a shopping list. I picked up the FPO book and put it in the briefcase, for the marina and store. "There's two clip boards. You want to learn how to do a subsistence survey?" I offered.

"Nope." George said.

That's my duty done. Fuck you. I spent a long day but got everyone who was home, that was all that was required by the O.P. Arriving at the boat I crawled in over the side after dropping in a box of groceries. George was finishing his supper. I greeted him with "Gas is paid for. I finished Tanana so we can leave in the morning." "Good." He said as he stowed groceries.

Am I really that hard to get along with? Just keep trying. Screw it.

After breakfast I said "I'll try something with the dishes I read about this summer after we get going. Let me get my hip boots on, I'll push us off. Unless you have a different plan my captain."

"Sounds right." George said.

Hip boots on, it took some heavy pushing, helped by the outboard to break the Wahoo free of where she had been sitting for over a week. As I finally pushed her out into the deep water for the first time I discovered climbing over the bow was more of a climb than I expected. Between sticky mud holding my feet, the boat pulling away and the height of the bow, I ended up half on and half hanging over the water, legs waving looking for a foothold. Through the windscreen over the cabin I could see a big smile on George's face. He was enjoying my plight. *The bastard.* My heel finally caught a gunwale and I pulled myself on to the bow. *Probably was pretty funny to watch. If I tried thinking positive thoughts he might come around. Power of positive thinking, someone wrote a book about that.* I worked my way around the cabin to the working deck. Not an easy task, not one to try in heavy weather. The narrow passage ways between the gunwales and the sides of the cabin were only about four or six inches wide. Safest way seemed to be to lean forward over the cabin roof while walking the gunwale, with your toes. *If I get the boat ready next year should add handrails.* I dropped on to the deck and walked over to George where he was standing at the steering station.

"Beautiful day. Should be a smooth trip to Kokrines." I said.

"Do we stop there?"

"Don't really need too. According to Reardon's notes it's just a fish camp now. They caught some people there who were still berry picking. But almost everyone had gone home with their fish. We're supposed to stop in case anyone stayed for fall chums and are striping roe." I said.

"They put salmon eggs up?" George asked.

"No, that was the big excitement when I was in Fairbanks. Governor issued an emergency regulation allowing people to sell the roe from subsistence fish. Some people are just striping the roe to sell and dumping the fish. We're supposed to watch for it." I explained.

"Are you going to arrest people?" George sounded concerned.

"Hell no. Just supposed to document it so they have evidence of why it shouldn't be legal. Right now, they aren't really breaking any law, except wanton waste, which is really hard to prove if the only evidence is a dead fish on the bottom river." *He doesn't say much. I **should shut up.***

"Hey captain, swing in close to that cut bank that's dripping with melting ice." I said as a black cut bank came into view.

"Why?"

"That's a well-known melting ice lens. For some reason, flood followed by freeze probably, there are a bunch of ice age critters thawing out there. People who've been here say you can actually smell the rotting meat. If you're lucky and the first one to pass by after its exposed, you can get some mastodon ivory or one guy I knew at the U had a giant bison skull he found." *So much for keeping my mouth shut.*

"It does stink." George confirmed.

I had my binoculars out studying the melting riverbank closely hoping for a fossil. All I got was a photo of a muddy river bank.

I got the dirty dishes from breakfast and put them in a nylon mesh bag I had picked up with the groceries. Tied it shut then put a rope threw the drawstring loop. Dropped it over the side and maneuvered it back into the prop wash of the mighty thirty-three horse Johnson outboard that was pushing us downstream. "There" I told George, "if the magazine was right we'll have clean dishes in half an hour. Probably still want to give them a rinse with boiling water. I don't think the river water is very clean."

"Humph."

"I'm going forward to read, holler if you need me." I ducked into the cabin, finished unzipping my sleeping bag and opened it up on the bunk to air out. Then, book in hand, binoculars and camera around my neck, I opened the hatch in the center front of the cabin and climbed out. Took a reclining position with my back to the slanted cabin bulkhead and started reading. Remembering my father's commands of "Trim up the boat." I choose the side opposite the steering station so my weight counter balanced

George's. Sun was warm, the book interesting, the engine soon lulled me into a pleasant state.

I checked the dishes when I finished a chapter. They were clean. There was no sign of life at Kokrines so we continued down the river. This was the life.

44 Magnum

After doing the subsistence survey in Ruby, the Wahoo continued downstream. When the sun went down we ducked into a side sloughs and anchored for the night. I pulled the anchor the next morning after our usual breakfast of fried bacon and eggs. Another beautiful day as we proceeded down the river. I sat out on the front deck, leaning back against the doghouse and reading. Frequently looking up to view the passing river and the surrounding boreal forest. I was reading the Koran as part of my spiritual journey. I was noticing many similarities to the Bible. *Plagiarism?* Suddenly the Johnson thirty-three gave a terrible bang, followed by silence and the vibrations through the Wahoo stopped. I put a bookmark in the Koran and opened the hatch to the cabin tossing the book on my bunk. I followed the book into the cabin but continued through to the work deck where George was bent over the engine. The engine was smoking a little.

"It's seized." He announced.

"Drifting with the current seems like a peaceful way to travel." I said as I moved to get the twenty-five horse Evinrude lashed to the starboard side, our spare powerplant.

"Get the spare." George said still looking and poking the dead engine.

Yes, my captain. No sense of humor. All business. "Yes" **don't say sir.** *Your right, why waste good sarcasm.* "Probably take both of us to lift the thirty-three off the transom." I replied untying the spare.

George was already unhooking the steering cables from the motor and didn't reply.

I unlashed the spare twenty-five horse Evinrude.

"Watch out." George warned.

I turned, he had the engine in both hands. His back bowed in a great effort and the engine actually moved up the transom but not far enough. With a grunt and a thump, it dropped back down. The mighty thirty-three Johnson was too much for George.

"Are you all right?" *Geez, that would be great to be drifting downstream with a guy with a back injury.*

"Yeah, going to take both of us." George confirmed my earlier remark.

Ya think! I stepped in next to him and we each took a grip, fore and aft on opposite sides of the engine. Our faces nose to nose over the engine. "On three." George said. "One, two, three"

"Humph!" we said almost simultaneously. It's impossible to coordinate exactly on "three" because the person counting knows when their saying three while the other has to wait for it. We did pretty well considering our lack of previous coordinated actions. We managed to lift the clamps off the transom and pulled the outboard into the boat.

"Wow, that outboard wasn't designed for mobility." I lifted my head and made a scan of our location in the river. "Looks like we're good for a while yet, but the current is pulling us towards the bank. Better get the spare on quick."

George was also looking. "Yep"

I handed the much lighter twenty-five to George over the thirty-three, lying dead on the deck. Not waiting for me he stepped back towards the transom with the twenty-five. Both of us were walking like drunks due to the boat rocking because of all the shifting weight.

"George, let me tie a safety line on the motor before you put it over the transom." I said. He didn't wait. *You drop it in the river and were rowing!*

He held the engine over out over the water, lowering the clamps onto the transom. *That's a relief.* We each tightened a clamp. The river bank was growing closer. I tied off the safety line. George stepped in with a gas hose, plugging it into our new power plant. He began pulling the starting rope so we would have control again. Which was becoming urgent as we clearly were going to run into the river bank.

I grabbed the oar. It was an ancient eight-foot oar, whatever finish it had once had was gone. It was so dry it was shedding splinters; the Wahoo didn't have oar locks. The oar's two purposes were to push off when leaving the shore and to meet the Coast Guard's minimum equipment requirement. I went forward, crouching through the cabin to the bow as quickly as I could. *Is this oar strong enough to fend the Wahoo off in this current?* As the bow swung into the bank, I adjusted my position to fend off the starboard bow, bracing my feet against the anchor and cabin. Just before striking, the bank came within range and I jammed the oar into the bank.

Just like Queequeg, except this is a mud bank not a sperm whale.

The blade of the oar sank into the dirt, as shaft began to follow it hit something solid. The bow swung out, pulling the oar through my hands. My grip failed as the splintery oar shaft bloodied my hands. *Damn splinters. Should have grabbed a pair of gloves. Dad's goanna get blood*[51]. *Whoa, where we going.* The force of my push and the current caused the boat to spin. The oar was jerked out of my hands. *That would have been one dead whale.* I scrambled aft, knowing I could never arrive in time to fend off the stern. *Fend it off with what?*

A lucky swirl in the current swung the Wahoo's bow too midstream so fast I had to grab the cabin walls to keep from falling. As I bounced through the cabin door I heard the welcome sound of the twenty-five coming to life. George was hugging the outboard like drunk hugs the head, to keep the swinging boat from throwing him overboard. His right hand came free, finding the throttle on the steering arm. The cold engine coughed as it received more gas than it was ready for but kept running. The prop dug in, adding a new direction to the forces trying to throw us to the deck. I fell backwards, saved by the cabin door. Our forward motion finally overcame the other motions. Grabbing a round five-gallon can of Blazo, I slid it to George to use for a seat. The steering wheel hadn't been reconnected to the replacement motor so he needed a place to steer from.

"Thanks, you hold her here. I'll hook up the steering cables." George commanded. "Geez, what happened to your hands?"

I looked at my hands, which were covered with blood, which dripped on the deck.

"Splinters from that fucking oar. It's buried in the riverbank. Let's just leave the damn thing and buy a new one in Galena." *Is that enough blood to satisfy?*

"Geiger won't like that. We'll go back."

"The fucking budget can stand a fucking oar. It's covered in my fucking blood. That makes it fucking mine. I say we leave it for some fucking anthropologist to dig up and wonder where it fucking came from."

---

[51] My father, always said a repair was no good unless you shed a little blood making it.

My hands were really stinging and my grip on the steering tiller was so slippery I was having trouble with the throttle.

George looked up from tightening the port steering cable. "We're going back." *Fuck you!*

George finished connecting the steering, throttle, and gear shift cables as I kept the Wahoo pointed upstream in mid-channel. My constant little course corrections to hold our position made his job harder. Every time my grip had to tighten I found a new splinter or my hand slipped in blood. I maliciously took my pain and anger out on George by timing my course corrections for the worst possible moment for the completion of his tasks. He patiently made all the connections evidently not realizing my evil actions or choosing to ignore them. ***Your being really rotten and childish. Straighten up.*** George finished tightening the cables. It looked a little sloppy, with extra cable sticking out, but it worked. We had control. George took over at the steering wheel and added full throttle.

"Hey, you were right, we ought to go back for the oar. Sorry, I was just pissed off about all these fucking splinters." I said as I looked at my mangled palms. I pulled my Swiss Army knife from my pocket. Getting blood all over my pants. The tweezers were worthless on most of the splinters; couldn't get a tight enough grip. I found the blade point usually could be inserted in the splinter enough to pull it out. *Just like Mom's needle.*

George turned the boat upstream towards the cut bank that was almost out of sight now. After what seemed like a long time working on my hands I looked up, if we had moved I couldn't tell.

"Are we making any headway at all?" I asked.

"Not much, the current is too strong for this motor." George replied.

Wow, his sentences are getting longer. Maybe this will work out. "We're spending more of the state's money on our wages than a new paddle will cost, let's hang it up." I added.

Nature decided I was right.

"A little longer." George said.

"OK"

Digging around in the first aid kit I found mercurochrome. *Shit. Mom use to put that on my splinters. Disinfects but it burns like hell.*

"Shit, fuck, damn it all." My left hand was red with the mercurochrome. I was waving it franticly trying to cool the burn. George was smiling at the wheel of the boat.

Enjoy, your right, I deserve this. I waved my left hand until it was dry and the pain subsided. The right was harder since I'm right handed. But lots of profanity and waving, it was done. I considered the wounds and the collection of bandages. *Think it's best to keep em as clean as possible and forget the bandages. Use the work gloves from now on dumb shit.*

We pulled into the boat beach, mud not sand, at Galena. I jumped ashore with the anchor securing the Wahoo. George was on the bow with the briefcase.

"You'll need this to call Geiger." He said handing it to me.

Isn't calling for a replacement outboard part of running the boat? **Don't ask.** "Ok, I'll find out where a phone is." Taking the brief case, I headed up the bank to the dirt road running along the river. A shabby windowless plywood building had a sign proclaiming it to be a bar and grill met my eyes. *They'll know where a phone is. Gosh a cold beer would feel good on my hands.*

Geez, dark in here. Probably the bright sun outside.

I stumbled to the bar and asked "Hi, is there a phone I can use?"

The bartender gave me a "you are stupid" look and pointed at the payphone on the wall between the end of the bar and the door to the pool room. There was one guy on the phone and several waiting impatiently at the nearest table.

"I'll have a draft please." I said to bartender. *How else do you wait in a bar?*

He pulled me the smallest glass of beer I've ever seen. "Two bucks"

Geez, I can buy a six pack of beer in Fairbanks for that. **You're not in Fairbanks.** I gave him two dollars. Went to the table where one of the waiting crew got up to make his call as the guy on the phone left.

"Where's the end of the line?" I asked trying to sound as friendly.

"After that guy." Said one of the rough looking bunch. I sat down next to That Guy. *Wow, I thought I was a little rough looking. Wonder how long these guys have been in the bush. That Guy, is drinking straight up whiskey, doesn't look like he'll stay upright till his turn. How will I handle that?*

"What do you guys do when not waiting for the phone?" I asked the table.

They all returned glares, except That Guy, who continued staring into his glass between swallows.

Guess no one is interested in conversation. I opened my briefcase and checked my subsistence survey list. Not many folks to see in Galena. Reardon and Allo got most of them. I studied the crowd in the bar. Most tables seemed occupied by groups who were talking together very freely. Evidently it was the phone table that was silent. Two fellows were playing darts. People were occasionally passing into the back room where the sound of pool balls hitting one another emanated. Not a woman in the place. The line was moving quickly most of the phone calls seemed to be brief. That Guy rose unsteadily when his turn came. He was wearing a large knife and a holstered revolver.

Wonder what caliber and make it is? Is he hunting? That might explain the knife and gun. That knife is way too big for cleaning game. Went that route once. Use Dr. Neiland's recommended Herter's knife now. He's not having much luck with his call. Wish he'd give up, fuck he's drawing his gun!

I slide low in my chair as That Guy backed away from the phone screaming "Fucking God Damned Phone" KER POW! I slide to the floor under the table. "Damn phone company." KER POW!

Should I tackle him by the feet? KER POW! *No one is screaming. We all seem to be under tables or behind the bar.* KER POW! *Best to wait till he's empty.* KER POW! *Should be over.* KER POW. *He doesn't carry safely on an empty chamber.*

I scrambled on all fours under the table towards his boots but was stopped by a stampede of booted feet. *I wasn't the only one waiting for him to empty his gun.*

That Guy was easily subdued in his drunken condition. I righted my chair and sat down my knees suddenly rather weak. I still had half a beer which disappeared in a single chug.

"You're a cool one." A stranger standing nearby said.

I nodded his way and gave him a small salute with my empty glass. *Don't dare speak, my quavering voice would give me away. Thought chugging booze was supposed to help.*

Maybe it has to be hard stuff. Look at the phone. Won't be making any calls on that sucker. Think I can talk now. I turned to my admirer and asked "Are there any other phones in town?"

"Out at the airport, but it's a long walk." He answered. Still can't believe you just sat there through all the shooting."

"Yeah, thanks." *That's why he thinks I'm cool. <u>Missed you jumping onto the floor.</u>* I got up, legs were working so to satisfy my curiosity I walked over to the back-room door and looked in.

Wow, those guys are back to their pool. Look at the wall, all those slugs went clear through into the pool room. Still they play. Now that's cool. I headed for the door, stopped and walked to the bar.

"Hey do you want my name as a witness?" I asked the bar tender.

"Witness to what?" he snarled.

Ok, so nothing happened. My imagination. Must be a good customer. Alaska still is the wild frontier. I checked the rough map of Galena in my briefcase and headed out towards the airport. Accepting my new Galena cool I stopped at two houses along the way I was supposed to survey. Easy ones. Both Kass'aks, husbands were moose hunting and wives didn't know how many fish they had caught. Didn't offer coffee, tea or baked goods either.

The airport terminal was pretty nice compared to Bethel's, which was a larger town. *Guess having an air force base helps.* I spotted three payphones on a wall by the baggage claim chute. *Wow, big time even has a little privacy wall between the phones. Very little privacy, look to be two by three feet. What would Superman do?*

After depositing a quarter, I got the operator and told her it was a collect person to person call to Mike Geiger. Gave her the number and listened while she called. A woman answered "Department of Fish and Game. How may I direct your call?"

"Collect person to person call for Mike Geiger from Kim Francesca. Will you accept the charges?" asked the operator.

"Please hold."

Interesting clicking sounds. *Wonder if they charge for the time all this is going on.*

Geiger's voice said "Hello". The operator explained Kim Francesca was calling collect from Galena would he accept the charges. There was a long pause. I figured Geiger was deciding if he knew a Francesca. He said "Yes, I'll accept the call."

"Hi Mr. Geiger its Kim Francisco."

"What's up?"

"The thirty-three-horse seized up. George says we need a new motor. The twenty-five is working fine but it can't push us upriver." I explained.

"I'll see what we have and ship something out air freight. You guys wait there for it." Geiger said.

"OK"

"How are things going otherwise?" Geiger asked.

"When the motor seized I lost the oar fending us off the bank. We couldn't get back upstream to get it so we need an oar too. Should we buy it here or do you want to send one with the outboard?" I asked.

"I'll send one. Ship the old motor back. How's the survey going?" Geiger wanted to know.

"Fine, I enjoy talking to people. George stays on the boat but I guess we've worked out a system. Hey, it's a long way from the waterfront to the airport. How should we move the motors?" My long walked suddenly came back to me.

"Get a cab. Just write an FPO for the fare." Geiger said.

"OK" I said. *Do they have cabs in Galena?*

"Anything else?" Geiger asked.

"Ugh, no can't think of anything. We'll watch for the outboard." I answered.

I cleaned up the last of the surveys on the walk back from the airport. *Another beer would be nice. What's all the hollering about? That's a beautiful Cessna 185 on floats parked next to us. Wish I could afford one. That's whose hollering. Local guys upset with the out-oftown hunters from the plane. Moose belong to everyone, locals disagree. "Tragedy of the Commons" Barry someone wrote that. Things look a little exciting. Hope no more guns are pulled. I've had my fill of gun play. Those guys want George to do something about the outof-towners. Better pass on the beer. George ducked out of sight.*

"Whose out there?" A vicious voice greeted me as I climbed over the bow rocking the Wahoo.

"Just little old me?" I answered.

"Who?" Demanded George, as he came out of the cabin with a hammer. "O, why didn't you say who you were. Things have been pretty hot here and they're trying to get me to do something because I'm Fish and Game."

"That happens in villages when you're the only authority figure. Galena must have cops, they'll show up soon. I hope. Of course, I didn't see any when that guy blew away the phone." I answered George.

"Get the anchor and let's get out of here." George said.

"OK, but we can't go far. Have to come back to see if the new outboard is here tomorrow, we can't go upstream." I gave an incomplete summary of my call.

"Let's go." George insisted.

I jumped down and grabbed the anchor and pushed the Wahoo off.

"Hey, where you going? God damn it, you need to protect my plane!" Hollered a guy standing on the plane's float.

"Sorry we're not cops. Sleep in the plane or move it." I hollered over the twenty-five's whine. *Not very helpful but what can I say. At least my voice didn't break.*

"Fuck you." From the plane.

"Thanks" Our pleasant conversation was ended by the twenty-five's shift into forward and full throttle. George turned upstream staying near the bank. This was a quiet area where we weren't fighting the full strength of the current so we could go upstream, rather slower than I would have liked. We were still in rifle range. At the top of the bend George headed out across the river, crabwise, that is the bow was pointing upstream enough that we didn't go downstream but across enough that we were moving across the current sideways. The way a crab walks. Watching land marks behind us I was concerned that we might be losing ground downstream but we made it across the thaweg and gained some lost upstream distance. We hit quiet water near the far shore. George was able to move the bow to point across and we pulled into the mouth of the slough on the other side of the river.

"George, drop me off on the bank. I'll take the shotgun and see if I can come up with some fresh meat." I said instead of anchoring the voice.

"Won't be anything this close to the village." He replied but dropped me off.

Wearing my hip waders and carrying the Browning Featherweight, a 20-gauge semiautomatic shotgun, I had purchased four years ago with the money I got for high school graduation. It had been a tough deal. After saving ten percent of the money in the Cisco Fund. As had been my custom since I was about twelve and listened to the "Richest Man in Babylon", a self-improvement record album Dad had brought home. I was about twenty bucks short of the asking price. Dad took me downtown in Des Moines to an Army/Navy surplus store he did business with. He coached me to look at the gun but not to eagerly then offer $40 less than the asking price. In spite of my best effort to look disinterested I was in love. Holding my dream gun was almost better than June's kiss. Desperate, almost in tears, I said "I only have $210 from graduation gifts."

The man smiled and said "Sold" then turning to my father "Dick you probably would have beat me out of at least the forty maybe sixty more."

Dad looked at me disappointed, a look I knew well, "Son you're going to have learn to not be so obvious. Never give away your top price."

Aw well, she's a beauty and has served me well. This is great, to be in the middle of the Alaskan wilderness, sneaking along a slough, looking for game for supper. Another meal of canned pork is too much. Steller's Jays, poor Steller, guess the official common name is now gray jay. Wonder if they'll take his name off everything he described. Careful sneaking around this curve, low and slow. Stop. Ducks. Wigeon, true subsistence hunter would take the shot on the water. **Be sportsman, step out, shoot em on the wing.** Bang, Bang, Bang *Wow, my first triple, no one to see it. Doesn't matter, you did it, three shots, three birds on one flush. Shit I don't have a dog. How will I get them? Should have thought of that dummy.* Luckily, unlike the Yukon Delta, the central Yukon is in the boreal forest zone of Alaska so a long stick was handy. Some quick trimming with my knife, presto a Shepard's crook. I wadded out into the slough towards the closest duck. With a reach I was able to drop the stick onto the drake Wigeon and pull him to me. I tossed him on the bank behind me and tried for the next. The very tip of my branch touched him, causing the bird to move a little further away. I wiggled and pulled my feet free of the mud, one at a time, taking another step closer. This time the hook I had improvised on the stick came down on the far side of the second duck and I was able to pull him in. Freeing my feet, I waded ashore, collected my two ducks and walked opposite the furthest one that was slowly drifting downstream and across the slough. I waded out until the water was an inch from the top of my waders.

Stretching and reaching as far as possible I couldn't reach the duck. I pulled my feet from the mud, wading ashore. Couldn't find a rock, but collected several short fat pieces of sticks, then waded out as close as I could get again, with my crook stuck down the back of my jacket. I tossed my throwing sticks so they landed just past the duck, most of them at least. The sticks created ripples that gently moved the duck in my direction. Drawing my crook after my last throw, *Just like Conan's broadsword.* I once again stretched until it hurt but still couldn't snag the duck.

We don't kill what we don't eat. Don't waste game. Father's admonitions ran through my brain so I took another step. Over topped one hip boot which filled with water. *Fuck it, I'm wet now. Frist rule of hip boots, their never high enough.* I waded on in and snagged the hen wigeon. I dropped her in my pocket then wadded towards shore. *Must have ten gallons in each boot. Just roll the tops down while wading out to drain part of it. Get em off now. Pour out the water. Hard as hell to get the wet boots back on. Let's see these birds. Two drakes, but they're not real pretty, coming out of eclipse plumage. Poor hen. Sorry little lady, you were just next in line. I'm not good enough to just shoot drakes particularly in eclipse plumage. Easier to just shoot rooster pheasants but ducks just don't look that different, but there are guys who just shoot drakes. Interesting management. Harvest all males in species where it's easy to tell em apart but if you can't then watch out girls. Wonder if it really makes a difference? Maybe species with lots of sexual dimorphism have large harems so bias in sex ratio towards males increases total production. Something to think about. Need to check the literature.* I got back to the boat as the sun was coming down. Hollered to George. Who started the engine. Left it idling while he pulled the anchor, then putt-putted back to pick me up. I climbed aboard and dropped the anchor when George had returned to midchannel.

"Well is in ham or bacon tonight?" George asked.

"Neither, fresh duck, I got my first triple." I said, pulling the birds out of my pockets.

"Huh"

"A triple in wing shooting, is when you get three birds out of a flush with three shots." I explained.

"So."

"You ever shot a shoot a flying target?" I asked.

"No but should be simple with a scatter gun." George answered.

"Well it's not. I'm not a very good shot, but a triple is a pretty big deal for the best shots.

Especially, with only a 20 gauge." I added.

"Most people I know use a 12 gauge. Must be easier with your bigger gun." George answered, showing he didn't know shotguns.

I laid the birds out for cleaning. I had hung my hip boots upside down and inside out on the gunwales to dry while we talked. Letting my pants dry while I wore them.

"No. Twelve gauges are bigger than twenties. I guess if you're not use to shotguns the smaller number in the name makes it sound smaller. It's backwards because gauge is based on how many even lead balls you can divide a pound of lead into. That's also why shot size is backwards. It's based on how many pieces of shot you could make out of a pound so the bigger the number the smaller the shot." I explained, trying not to sound like I was talking down to George.

"So, your twenty gauge can't shoot as far as a twelve?" George asked.

"Even lots of shooters think that, but range of the shell depends on shot size. Bigger the piece of shot is, the further it can go. Like throwing feathers and rocks. The advantage of a twelve gauge over a twenty is the bigger shell allows more pieces of shot in the shell. Which causes a bigger-denser pattern further from the gun." I explained as I filleted the breasts from the ducks during our talk. Holding up two of the small pieces of meat I announced "Dinner".

George looked dubious.

"You'll see. It will be a nice change from all this canned pork." I took some pancake mix, we didn't have any flour, put it in a plate and dredged the breasts and tiny legs. Put a big dollop of bacon fat I had saved from the pound of bacon we had for breakfast and fried the duck. Being careful to take them off the heat while still pink in the middle.

George watching said "I prefer mine well done. Don't want to catch anything."

"You like tough liver?" I asked.

"No."

"Then you won't like well-done duck. There's nothing you can catch from ducks.[52] Here you go." I dropped three breasts on his plate.

George took a tentative bite, smiled and gobbled up his three breasts. He picked the tiny legs out of the frying pan and nibbled off the tiny pieces of meat. "These are hardly worth the effort."

"Yeah, I don't usually bother with the legs but thought we'd be hungry for a change in meat." I answered.

"Why didn't you shoot more?" He asked.

"I got wet retrieving these. It was getting dark. Wanted to come home to get dry and warm.

The beans are hot." I said.

We ate our pork and beans and barricaded ourselves in the cabin against the mosquitos. The next morning after bacon and pancakes we crossed the river again. Came in next to the 185 and discovered it resting, sunk on the bottom, the floats destroyed by axe cuts. The plane wouldn't be taking off for a while.

"Warned him to sleep in his plane. Heard of this kind of think happening to plane hunters out by Minto." I said.

"Where's Minto and how do you know this stuff?" George asked.

"I watch or listen to the news and read the paper, when I can afford one. Minto is a village on some lakes near Fairbanks." I replied.

"Don't like news." George said.

I was pulling on my hip boots. Still cold and a little damp from retrieving ducks. As George nosed the Wahoo into the bank I jumped off with the anchor but didn't pull the line tight, leaving a little slack. Then I wadded around to the stern which was swinging downstream with the current. I guided it in as tight to the bank as I could get it. Snugged the anchor line, which with the current made the Wahoo pretty stable against the bank. While I was busy with the Wahoo, George untied lines lashing the thirty-three to the side of the boat. I climbed back in and we each squatted on opposite ends of the motor. I had taken the lower unit.

"Took the light end." George said.

"My Mama didn't raise know fool." I answered.

"Thought you were weaker. Ready to lift?" George asked.

---

[52] That's not completely true.

"On three, one, two, three." We both lifted and the thirty-three rose to the gunwale, where we set it while we caught our breath.

"It hasn't gotten any lighter." I said to George.

"Nope. I'll hold it, you step out and I'll lower it to you." George said.

Maybe Mom did raise a fool. One who is about to be buried in mud by the weight of this outboard. I stepped over the side while George balanced the outboard on the gunwale. Then he pivoted the powerhead on the gunwale with the lower unit sticking out towards me. I took the lower unit and pushed down while George slowly relaxed his hold on the powerhead. The heavy motor pivoted on the gunwale as we both struggled to control our part so that it descended slowly. There were a few, exciting moments as various parts caught, were lifted or pushed free but almost like we knew what we were doing the engine dropped into my arms. I had the powerhead in my arms balancing the motor on its skeg. I tried to drag the motor up the bank but my feet were firmly trapped in the mud. "I'm stuck."

"Yeah." Said George, stepping over the side, smiling.

George and I exchanged arms, his replacing mine under the powerhead. He then backed up, dragging the thirty-three's skeg up onto the small mud beach. I finally freed my feet with a mighty sucking sound and staggered after him. Reaching down, I picked up the lower unit as he dragged. Resistance from the drag gone, we continued the few steps to the four-foot bank, kicking backward with his heels, George made steps in the soft bank as we climbed to the road. At the top we squatted in unison setting the motor down.

We dragged the motor a few yards from the edge of traveled portion of the waterfront road.

"We better head to the airport. I'll get a cab." I gasped.

"Will the boat be safe?" George asked, looking at the plane resting on the bottom.

You're not getting out of this trip into town. "We aren't moose hunting and its daylight so it should be alright. I'll go see if I can find a cab."

"I'll lock the cabin." George said. There was a padlock and hasp on the door.

Conveniently or perhaps not, a cab arrived and the pilot and his friends tumbled out, looking like they spent the night drinking, not sleeping.

"My plane. God damn the fucking bastards. I'll kill em." Pulling his pistol, he asked "Was it these bastards?" Gesturing with the barrel at a few on lookers who had gathered to watch us wrestle the engine.

I had moved up to the cab driver who was unloading his trunk. "Can you give us and that outboard a ride to the airport?"

"I'm talking to you, you fucking bastard, are you going to arrest someone?" Grabbing my shoulder, he spun me around. I turned back to the driver. *Shit, ignore him. Best plan?* The driver, confused, said "Yeah, but the outboard is full fare and you have to load and unload yourselves."

Grabbing my shoulder with one hand and waving the pistol unsafely with the other, the pilot spun me around screaming in my face "I'm talking to YOU!"

The driver dove into his cab. *Wish I could follow.* Backing up to the motor. George signaled him to stop, he was close enough. Then squatted and loaded the motor.

"You fucker, you were supposed to guard the plane last night. What do you have to say for yourself."

Our audience was growing. *What can I say? Where's the police?*

"You bastard, are you fucking going to answer me." I was standing stunned. He had a hand on each shoulder, the pistol grip digging into my left shoulder where his right hand held me.

One of his buddies was hovering behind him, indecisively, saying something I couldn't hear.

Damn, my ears aren't working. Whatever he said distracted the pilot, who let go of me and turned on him. George was free of the motor and moved up behind the pilot, making him seem smaller, if you forgot the gun in his hand.

Reinforcements freed my voice and hearing. "Sir, we did not agree to spend the night with your plane. We are conducting a subsistence survey for the Division of Commercial Fisheries. Guarding planes isn't in the operating plan." I said calmly. *Thanks for keeping the voice steady.* **Your welcome.**

Turning back to me the pilot said "You smart assed fucker, I'll kill you!" He raised both arms to grab me. Luckily forgetting the gun in his hand. I turned my body sideways, stepping into a boxing pose, fists closed, my left ready to block incoming punches. *Stupid, you don't use fists in a gun fight!* **Drop and roll.** Before thoughts became actions. George moved forward, the hovering buddy wrapped his arms around him from behind. Pinning his arms to his sides.

"They had left before we did! Don't get arrested for murder!" His buddy screamed in his ear.

Quivering with rage the pilot screamed "You bastard, which of these fuckers do I shoot?"

Still ready to box I said "Sir, we didn't see it happen. None of these men were here when we arrived. I would call the police if I were you." *Damn, quaver in my voice.*

"I'll fucking do that. I'll call your god damned boss too." The quivering pilot screamed.

Please don't let go of him. The cab driver had opened the doors on each side. George and I backed into our respective doors, dove in, closing them as quickly as possible. The cab pulled away. A glace back showed a very angry man still being controlled by his friends.

"You almost got killed?" George said.

"Can't blame him for being mad. Like the monkey said when he peed on the cash register "That's going to run into money." But why me." I said, finding relief in speech.

"He should know better than to come take our moose. Rich bastard." The driver added.

Takes his money to drive him around still doesn't think he has a right to hunt here.

Interesting.

"Where am I dropping you?" the driver finished.

"Wein Airfreight." My quivering voice said.

"OK"

George squatting and pressing then dropping the outboard into the trunk with his adrenaline pumping was one thing. Getting it out was a task. In the small space we couldn't get under it. The driver finally had to break down and help so he could take another fare. He wasn't really happy when I wrote him a FPO. "Good as money." I assured him. He didn't look convinced. Inside I filled out the shipping forms for Anchorage, my hands still shaking. The Wein folks tagged the motor, turned it upside down on a dolly and one small guy took it away to join the rest of the freight.

"We could've used one of those." I said watching the heavy old thing being handled easily by one man.

"Tires are too narrow for mud." George commented.

I called Geiger. It was brief, the new engine would be here today according to Wein. I told him the same about the old engine.

"George, we'll have to wait. Replacement is supposed to be coming in today. It's only a twenty-five horse so we'll have to run twin engines." I said, hanging up and turning to him.

Thank God, the quaver is gone.

"OK" George said.

We took seats. I so settled down to read the unfinished Koran. *Not as long as the Bible but it's still a long slog.* George alternately sitting, walking around, looking at in-flight magazines left lying around, passed the time. We had to wait until after lunch. Except we hadn't brought lunch. The airport only had vending machines but it's hard to beat Snickers and M&Ms for lunch. The replacement motor arrived. I signed all the papers while George untied the oar from the motor.

"Let's go get a cab." I said.

"We can carry this one." George said.

"Maybe you can carry it over a mile. I'm getting a cab." I said.

"No, we'll carry it." George commanded.

"Then you'll carry it by yourself." I said. *Maybe part of a boat, but terra firma my domain.*

"Fine, that's not a problem." George acquiesced.

"I'll take the oar." *Never say I didn't do the least I could.*

George made it through the door carrying the motor by the handle on the front. Then set it down.

"You ready for a cab now?" I asked. *Please be reasonable.*

"No, we don't need a cab." He squatted down grasping the motor fore and aft, lifted it onto his shoulder and stood up. "Let's go."

We hiked down the road towards the river. We did try carrying the motor between us suspended from the oar but couldn't make it work. George had to stop every quarter of a mile or so and shift the motor from one shoulder to the other. *I should take a turn.* **Why?**

Geiger said we could use a cab. We used one to get to the airport, why not for the trip back.

Nope he said he'd carry it. Let him carry it. My alter egos argued for the whole trip.

George was sweating profusely when we arrived at the boat.

"You did it. I'm impressed. Looks like you could use a beer. Come on, I'm buying." I suggested when we finally made the Wahoo.

"No thanks. Let's get out of here." George said. I didn't argue.

DEVIL WOMAN

Things ran smoothly after Galena. Koyukuk and Nulato went quickly. Kaltag, our next stop, I was really looking forward to. My friend from Emmonak, Ed Kallands, AC's bookkeeper's assistant, lived here and I was happy to renew our friendship. Little did I know before the day was done I would have my honor defended, twice; I would fight for my honor and the Wahoo would be hexed.

We had arrived in the morning, which was a good thing since for whatever reason Reardon and Coffee and missed a lot of people there. We beached the boat and I got my paperwork together.

"George, my first stop is going to be Ed's house. His wife postmistress, so they'll be able to give me the lowdown on everyone on the list. Nice folks, I'm sure you'd be welcome for a mug up." *If I can get you off the boat just might get you to do a survey or two.*

"No, need to find gas and clean the spark plugs." George announced his plan.

"Fine, your loss, the coffee cake will be better than our pilot bread. *George didn't like pilot bread.* They'll know where to get gas." I commented.

"No."

The post office was easy to find. One of the larger buildings. It was just a low roofed building, maybe thirty feet by thirty. Attached at the back was high roofed cottage style house. No sign of which came first. The front door under the Kaltag Post Office sign was open so I walked in. A bell over the door rang. It was so dark I couldn't see, then I remembered my sunglasses. *I can see again.* Small miracles always lighten my heart. I looked around and PO boxes lined one wall. There was a table in the center with pen and some basic postal supplies. *Just like any post office. All the other village P.O.s seemed to be a window in a wall. Ed does things right.*

I crossed to a door in the back wall. Before I could knock on the inner door, a service window next to it opened. A young woman asked "Can I help you?"

"Hi, I hope so. I'm Kim Francisco…"

"Bring him in." interrupted a familiar voice from inside.

The young woman disappeared, the door opened and I entered a dining room/kitchen. There was a large table were Ed sat with his coffee. The young woman passed behind him and on into the kitchen. Ed introduced me to his wife, the post mistress, Virginia. Who was coming out of the kitchen wiping her hands on a towel. A very pleasant but clearly busy woman. She seated me across from Ed, whom I shook hands with across the table. As I pulled my arm in a mug of coffee, fresh bread, coffee cake, Strawberry jam and butter were set before me by Ed's daughter, the young woman at the window. "Have you had breakfast?" Virginia asked. Clearly ready to whip me up a breakfast.

"No, thank you. Ate before we headed out this morning." "Where did you camp last night?" Ed asked.

"Just upriver a couple of miles. Miss read the map, thought we had further to go."

"So what adventures have you had on your river trip?" Ed asked.

I told Ed about my triple. He told me how his boys had been moose hunting unsuccessfully until he stepped in and insisted on going along.

"They do it all wrong. They spot a moose then roar down on it full speed, blazing away and not hitting anything but the trees because of the boat bouncing. The moose all disappear into the trees. I had them drop me off with my grandson at my favorite slough and sent them away.

We waited. Pretty soon a nice little mulligan[54] stepped out. I was using my seal rifle, 222 Remington and aimed for his lungs. I don't think he even heard the shot. His head was under.

He turned and shook like a fly bit him then kept sticking his head under water pulling-up plants.

About 20 minutes later he waded ashore with some difficulty. My grandson say's "Shoot grandpa he's getting away." "No, he's not" I answered. We waited where we were. You know I don't walk so well anymore. The boys came back with nothing I said "I got one. Take me down the slough I'll show you." We take the boat down, I send them ashore and there's the moose. Never knew he was shot." Ed finished.

Not sure a 222 is legal. Have to check. Not that it matters. No evidence or witness. "Guess your sons learned to be patient." I commented.

"Probably not, their young, like you, patience isn't in you yet. I didn't have any when I was a boy." Ed sagely added.

[5454] Young bull moose.

"I had a small moose adventure in Nulato. Only light on at my last house was in the smokehouse. I knocked, the door flew open nearly knocking me down. A man was butchering a skinned moose that was hanging there. A small boy, his son, had opened the door.

Hi I'm from Fish and Game I started but my usual explanation of why I was there being cut short by the man turning quickly, crouching, and holding the knife ready to attack.

"Hey, I don't care about the moose. I'm here to ask how many salmon you caught." My voice was trembling, I was scared.

The fiery glare in his eyes faded into a relaxed friendly look as he stood up and resumed skinning.

"My calendar hanging there." He gestured to the inside of the smokehouse door I was standing next too.

Turning and taking it down off its nail I asked if he wanted to keep it.

"Take. Why keep?" He said.

"Some people like too, so they can compare years. Looks like you had good luck moose hunting. That's great." I told him.

"Yeah, no meat on antlers."

That's why my "I'm Fish and Game" scared him. I hadn't noticed it was a cow. Glad I'm not a protection officer. Might be swimming with the salmon. It was a short sweet survey and

then I fled.

"Kim, you're going to get in trouble with the bosses one of these days. You can't ignore law breakers." Ed warned.

"Yeah probably. I could talk all morning but I do have some work to do. I think you can help me locate the houses I need to go to."

Virginia said "Do you have a list?"

"Yes, I have it all here." I opened the briefcase. "Here's my list. The names that are checked off were interviewed by the team who took the boat upriver. So, I just need to do the ones who are left."

We repositioned ourselves on either side of Ed, putting the list in front of him. He and Virginia scanned the list, checking a couple of names off and telling me they were deceased or had moved. Ed and Virginia added a couple of new subsistence fishers. *Great, more surveys.*

Giger will be happy. "Here you go." They had numbered the remaining names.

"The first house is the furthest from here, going upstream. It's about fifteen houses from here. Then just ask where the next house is when you're done. You'll be working downstream towards the post office. You can't go wrong." Ed explained.

"Thanks, this should speed things up." I said.

"You'll have dinner with us. Virginia said.

"I wouldn't miss it. There's another guy on the boat, is it OK if I invite him too?" "Sure, there will be plenty." Virginia answered.

Parting good byes all around and I walked out through the post office. George was coming out of the store, which was almost next door, so I asked him if he wanted to come to lunch. He declined. I headed for the first house.

Things went smoothly. Except, my intention of saving room for dinner[53]. It seemed I was expected everywhere. Not surprising, the CB network in the villages had increased the speed of the grapevine. Evidently a good word from Ed and Virginia carried a lot of weight. Seemed to be a competition to see who could give me the best snack and most coffee. I was sloshing along stuffed with coffee, tea, cinnamon rolls, coffee cake, and doughnuts with three houses left to do when I knocked on Cindy's door. Virginia had wanted to draw a line through it but Ed had stopped her. There had been a brief discussion in Athabascan and she stayed on the list.

The door opened and I made my usual opening remark "Hi, I'm Kim, with Fish and Game.

I'm here to pick-up your subsistence calendar."

"Come in, come in. I'll get it for you." I was lead to the table and took a seat. *Fortyish. Not plump, like most women of her age. Rather slender. Twenty years ago, she would have been interesting.*

After searching through a pile of papers she announced "I must have started a fire with it.

No husband or son so didn't fish. Got fish from friends." She informed me.

---

[53] Lunch for you city slickers.

"That's OK about the calendar then. Aw, err." *I looked down my list of questions. Don't need to ask if anyone else lived with her or if she got fish from someone else.*

"Thank you. That was all I needed. Thanks again." I stood-up and headed towards the door.

She quickly crossed to me "Please stay for coffee?"

"Thank you but no thanks. I've had coffee at every house I'm about coffee'd out. I'll go now." *Jerk, the poor women's lonely. What can I do?*

Her hand covered mine as I tried to open the door, she was pushing it closed.

"Stay with me. We'll have a real good time!" Her free arm went around my waist.

Whoa, this doesn't happen in real life. Maybe in Penthouse Letters but those are always young babes, not women twenty years older. I exerted my strength and pulled the door open.

She exerted hers pushing it closed. *Wow, she's strong.*

The door was finally open enough that I turned sideways, out of her hug and slipped a foot and leg into the small opening. This gave me the leverage to break Cindy's hold on the door. I stumbled onto the entryway and down the stairs. Cindy was right behind.

"Baby, if you stay, I can show you where there's all the gold you can carry. Nuggets you just pick-up out of the stream." She promised.

Yeah sure, all the prospectors that have combed this country missed it. You know where all this gold is but live in BIA housing[54].

I said "No thank you. I have a job and girlfriend," **Liar,** "so I'm good."

Cindy grabbed me and spun me around, then pressed herself into me, squirming sensually against me. I backed-up, trying to hold her away. *This finally happens but I'm not interested.* I escaped by pushing her away. She staggered but didn't fall, to my relief. I escaped to the stairway of the next house I was to survey. Knocking on the door, as Cindy grabbed at me and tried to turn me to face her again. The door opened and a tiny woman burst out with a broom. Whack. She let Cindy have it over the head. Whack, whack, whack she chased her off the porch, down the stairs and

---

[54] Bureau of Indian Affairs. Alaska only has two reservations. Most Native Alaskans live where they always have. BIA had programs that provided housing, education, and health care. But some people had the means to provide their own houses.

out into lane. Cindy retreated towards her house. The lady with the broom returned to me and said pleasantly as if nothing happened "Come in."

Glad the broom wasn't for me. Wow, never seen anything like that before. I was standing inside the door. My rescuer put the broom back next to the door. *For the next time?* She crossed into the kitchen and took the subsistence calendar from the wall but held it close.

"I have calendar but need for rest of month. You still take?" Concern in her voice.

"Err, no you can keep the calendar. Are you still fishing?" I asked.

"No, no. Done fishing but use calendar. Need get one from store next month." She explained.

"Guess I should tell the boss a calendar for the whole year would be good for some people." I said.

"Yes, that good."

"I need to copy the numbers or can I have the months that are done?" Puzzled look. "Not sure?" She said.

I put my hand out, "May I hold the calendar? She pressed it against her chest. "I'll show you. I'll give it back. I promise."

She handed the calendar reluctantly to me. No fish were recorded in September, but there were some other notes. I flipped the pages over so we were back at the first page for June.

"I would just take June, July and August. Just these three pages." I flipped through the pages back to September. "You can keep September. Unless you want to keep the whole calendar, then I'll just copy your fish catch into my notebook and give you the whole calendar back." I noticed the black and white drawings of the fish that decorated the pages had all been carefully colored in.

"Want whole calendar." She said, holding it tightly to her chest.

"OK, can I sit at the table to copy your numbers of fish?"

"Yes, coffee?" Smiling again and handing me the calendar.

Can I drink another cup? Hell, why not. It's polite. "Yes, please" I followed her to the kitchen table. I lay down the calendar and began copying catch numbers onto the catch form for her family. She brought the coffee, setting it next to my work area.

"Thank you, who did such a good job coloring the fish?" I asked.

"My son. He moose hunting with father." She said proudly.

"He's a great artist." I said.

Some small footsteps sounded behind me. I looked over my shoulder and two round little faces framed by black hair peeked around the corner from the hall. Turning in my chair to face them I said "It's alright, I don't bite, you can come out." One face disappeared back into the hall but the taller of the two came out tentatively. "Hi I'm Kim, what's your name?" She ran to her mother and hide, peeking out around her leg.

"She Lucy." Her mother said.

"Hi Lucy, you're a beautiful little girl." Her mother beamed as she walked with small steps so Lucy could hang on to her leg.

"Just finished baking." *O no!* She put down a loaf of bread that still gave off that marvelous fresh baked smell. Of course, the butter and jelly were already on the table. *Can't eat another bite. Hot bread, melted butter. Got to.*

"Thank you" I took a slice of the warm bread and spread soft butter on to it. The butter melted in and I took a bite. Swallowing the first bite I looked at the baker saying "This is great.

Thank you."

The smell overcame Lucy's fear of the stranger and she came up to the table reaching for the bread. Her mother fixed a slice with butter and jelly and seated her across from me. Her sister, jealous, hungry or both couldn't stay hidden, came running out for her slice. I was working at a table with two little girls, one in a high chair and one whose eyes just peeked over the edge from her seat on a chair. Her mother was sitting between the girls helping out as needed.

Finishing with the fish and my slice, I asked "I have a few more questions about your family, may I ask?"

"Yes"

I went into the questions about family size, how fishing was, did they get enough fish and such.

"That's it. Thank you for your help, your calendar was the best I've seen so far. Thanks for the bread and coffee and thank you young ladies," I looked down at the girls, "for your company."

The oldest one hid her face in her mother's lap. The littlest one just kept happily stuffing bread into her jelly smeared face. "Could you tell me where the Honea's house is?" I asked.

"Gone moose hunting. No one home." She answered.

"OK, thanks again." *That's it, doy.* We walked to the door. Grabbing the broom, she opened the door and looked around carefully.

"It safe, you leave." She said. "Bye, bye."

I walked down the stairs and headed towards the Post Office and lunch. *How the hell are you going to eat lunch, you pig. Your stomach sloshes when you walk from coffee and I'm so full I may puke. What!*

Cindy had me wrapped in her arms, in a strong grip. "Honey, all women in Kaltag hate me cause their men love me. Feel how strong I am. Cut fish all day, make love all night." She pulled herself against me again sensually twisting against me. "I make you rich and happy. Stay one winter. Then go with gold."

Geez, what can I fucking do. Can't assault a woman. Try prying her off. Probably quite Kaltag's entertainment today. Where's my friend with her broom. I carefully pulled one of Cindy's arms free. *She's not lying about being strong. Fuck you lady, let go! That's all she wants. Don't need your help.* "Please let go. I can't spend the winter. I already paid my tuition, **lie,** for this fall. Classes start soon and I have to get back. I love my girlfriend." *Gon'a start lying, may as well be all in.* I whined then pried myself free and started speed walking for Ed's.

Cindy was circling me saying loudly "Women call me Devil Woman; their men enjoy me that much." She said darting around me trying for an opening to reestablish her grip. I used my arm and briefcase to block her grabs.

"Wouldn't having me around cramp your style?" I asked.

She stopped, falling behind as I hurried to the post office door.

Question worked. Wonder if she stopped trying to understand it or considering how boring just one guy would be?

Cindy was back, a little out of breath, grabbing my arm as I went into the post office. I may have been right about the show, Virginia seemed to be waiting just inside the door. She suddenly appeared to be a foot taller as she laid into Cindy.

"You get out! You only come to pick up your mail! Otherwise keep out! No mail for you!" Cindy vanished. *Wonder if "no mail" statement of fact or threat? Maybe she meant male?"* I was already at the inner door. A steaming Virginia stomped across the post office muttering in Athabascan and English, I understood "that woman" as she went through the door I was holding open. Ed hadn't appeared to move since that morning but looked as if he might explode suppressing his laughter. Now that I was safe, it seemed funny too but I followed Ed's lead and didn't laugh. *Wonder what the guys in the dorm will say about passing up sex?*

Virginia, normal sized, with a pleasant smiling face, turned and said "I'm sorry. That terrible woman, shame of Kaltag. No one else is like that."

"I agree. Everyone was kind and welcoming, you have a wonderful village here." *Cindy was welcoming too, in her way. I'll sure will never forget Kaltag.*

"Sit down" Ed said indicating a chair opposite him.

I took the chair by the back and said "If you don't mind, think I'll stand for a while. Been sitting all morning." *Hope all this food settles into my legs.* "I actually could use the bathroom.?"

"Lots of coffee? Over there." He pointed at a door behind me.

I stepped in and was a little surprised. Instead of a small space with just enough room for the bucket it was a "real" bathroom. *One of the advantages of living in a former trading post?* Some concessions to the lack of running water, a large bucket with a dipper sat on a threelegged stool for water. There was a wash basin and mirror, soap in a dish. Towels on a towel rack. A bathtub. *Must have to bring hot water from kitchen.* The walls had decorative wallpaper. And of course, a honey bucket, sitting where the toilet would have been. After a long refreshing draining of my bladder. I closed up the lid. Then put the plug in the washbasin, followed by a dipper of water and washed my hands well with the rough Lava soap bar and went out to lunch.

At least I can fit in another cup o joe. Hope there is softer soap for baths.

Ed's daughter brought out a basket of fresh baked dinner rolls which she offered to me first, as the guest. I almost said no thank you but familiar smell of fresh baked yeast touched my greedy spot and I soon was watching butter melt into the hot roll. Virginia brought out a white porcelain covered dish. She took the cover off in front of me and steaming there was chicken and dumplings. The dumplings all snug in the gravy. *Full stomach be damned.*

The sight and smell brought back many suppers at home and my grandmother's. I dug in. I just love dumplings, even though I've fixed them and know they are only flour, water and a dab of grease. There wasn't much conversation during the meal. I was the last one finished. *Chew every bite twenty times. Kindergarten? Worked, most food disappears in my mouth. Is this swallow going to come back up?*

Ed finished and asked me "How the trip was going?"

Swallowing I answered "Great, can't believe I'm getting paid to do this. Most of the time.

That's quite a collection of artifacts you have there." There was a barrister's bookcase behind him filled with a collection of arrowheads, baskets and even a jade bear spearhead. Allo had told me about them.

"Yes, I've been picking them up all my life. Archeologist from U of A was here a few years ago took a couple of hours going over them. He was disappointed they weren't in place. He had one they found digging near here he asked me about. It was an ivory harpoon head, like you saw in Emmonak." Ed explained.

"All of them I saw were made from steel, out of old outboard prop blades." I replied.

"Yeah, this one was a beauty. Ivory, like this one." He reached into a shelf and handed me an ivory harpoon. Both blade and socket carved from walrus ivory. I tested the point, still sharp.

"He wanted to know what people this far upriver would hunt with a harpoon? "Nothing" I said. "That's not a real harpoon point but one made for trading." He said "It's a harpoon head, see how the point fits into the socket." "Yes" I said.

"But its missing the most important part." Ed said.

I rechecked. "No, it's all here."

"Nope, you missed the same thing the archeologist did, it doesn't have a hole for the buoy line." Well, that stumped the professor and he looked at the head for a long time. Then he said "I'll be damned your right. This would never work. Why did they spend so much effort making it?"

"Because who ever made it knew when he crossed the mountains on the Unalakleet/Kaltag trail some Athabaskan would like it and trade for it. Did you think we only traded for stuff we could use? We're all people. Do the same things."

He said "Thank you very much. You just taught me an important lesson in Archeology. I'll have to use this point to teach my students to observe carefully and remember people are people."

I was finally finished eating. *You're really finished. Probably can't move without throwing up. Hell, I'm in no hurry. Just rest and talk a while.* "I went to an Archeology lecture where the professor taught pretty much the same thing. He told how they were mapping all the broken spear and arrow head points they found at a site. They made a semi-circle around the stone napping spot, where the stone worker sat. He and the students were discussing why a semi-circle of broken points; religion, custom, they couldn't figure it out. A laborer from the job site had wandered over and was looking in and listening.

He said "You over-educated fools, it's the O hell line." Insulted they asked what that was? He answered "Your sitting there chipping away for hours, you make a mistake and ruin the arrowhead you're working on. You take it and throw it as far as you can, saying "O hell". You end up with the semi-circle that's on you map."

Being good scientists, they tested the idea and sat at the napping site and threw arrowhead sized rocks. They all landed in the semi-circle. People are people, you don't want to over think this stuff." I told Ed.

"You tired of Alaskan strawberries on the boat yet?" Ed asked.

Strawberries! Haven't seen a strawberry patch since I left Iowa. The Commons serves them rarely. Where would Ed get strawberries? How'd we go from archeology to fruit? "No, hope they're their desert." *I'll explode but strawberries!*

"We don't have strawberries but we do have fresh cake still warm from the oven."

Virginia said, as her daughter put down big pieces of devil's food cake with chocolate frosting and scoops of vanilla ice cream on the side.

Gluttony, the deadly sin that will undo me.

As we dug in Ed explained "Alaskan strawberries is what we called red beans in territorial times. Main stay of everyone's diet in those days."

"I thought maybe you had a patch hidden out back. In Plant Morphology last year, we heard about a botanical survey then did near Fort Yukon and they were amazed when they found a patch of wild strawberries. They found some other surprising plants. When they got back to the U and were doing their research for the paper announcing this great discovery, they found out that the Department of Agriculture had abandoned an experimental farm where they found the plants. Some plants hung on. Surprising, since I know some people in Fairbanks that have worked really hard at raising strawberries with just a few to show for it." I explained.

"Those scientists should have brought a few back. They must be a tough enough strain by now. Then we would have Alaskan strawberries." Ed said.

"Publish or perish, sometimes thinking about the paper their going to write gives people tunnel vison. I thought they should have brought some back too. That's why I asked about a patch out back. Thought we could go partners and make a dollar or two." I said.

"Kim, do you know what happens to that information you ask for about families?" Ed's daughter asked.

Swallowing, "Ugh, no not really. I think they use it so they can estimate how many fish the families we don't interview catch. Geiger did tell me they keep it confidential so individual's information can't be picked out."

"Why do they care about subsistence fish?" She asked.

"That one I know. Geiger explained how they manage the commercial and subsistence fishery. Ed might remember but I guess back in the twenties or so the Feds opened a commercial fishery at the mouth of the Yukon. There weren't enough fish upriver for subsistence and there was a serious famine so they closed it down and it never reopened until statehood." I replied.

"I remember. I was working on the steamboats, lots of people hungry because not enough fish. It was bad." Ed said.

"The state took over and started the subsistence surveys and made a SWAG about how big the total run was. Then set the harvest guidelines for the commercial fishery. They need to keep track of subsistence catch so they can increase or reduce the commercial catch."

"What's a swag?" asked someone.

"Excuse me, scientific slang. It's an estimate when you don't know very much. The nick name for scientific wild ass guess, SWAG." I explained.

Everyone laughed. "Is it still SWAG?" Ed asked.

"No, they have quite a few years of data now so the estimate is much better. Geiger says using the well-kept calendars he was able to figure out the speed of migration, looking at peaks in each village. When they did tagging studies, they found the same speed." I said.

"Then why tag?" Ed asked.

"They get a lot more than just speed from the tags. Population estimate, find new spawning streams, separate Canadian fish from Alaskan fish. That's what I was doing before I started the survey. Tagging fall chums in Rampart so they can figure out how many are Canadian for the negotiations."

"What are you going to do after the subsistence survey?" Virginia asked.

"Gee, not sure right now. I don't have classes until January, so I might go trapping, once the season opens. Draft board might want me to be in school so I might enroll late and take some fun courses. Might do some traveling in the lower forty-eight. *Look for June. Nah, don't say that.* Don't know yet."

"What about that girl in Emmonak?" Ed asked.

"She dumped me as soon as she got back to school in Seattle for another guy. She's not my plan anymore." *Felt good to finally say it out loud to someone. Draining the festering wound, I guess.*

"To bad, thought you two were good with each other." Ed said.

"Yeah, I still really miss her. But to be fair, she never did say she felt the same way I did.

Life goes on, as my father said "Women are like buses, there's another along every ten minutes." Ed chuckled but Virginia and her daughter gave me the evil eye. "No buses along the Yukon though." Ed really laughed but the evil eye got worse.

Thought that would help. Didn't. Better shut up, better they feel sorry for me.

"Guess George will be wondering what happened to me. Thank you for a wonderful lunch and conversation. George and I don't talk much." *Confessions just pouring out.*

"Did he work with you in Emmonak?" Virginia asked.

"No, I just met him in Tanana. Guess he was a transfer from somewhere but he's never mentioned where. He's good with the boat and motors but won't do survey work." I said.

"Why not?" Ed's daughter asked as she was picking up my dishes.

"I'm not sure, but I think he's afraid of villagers but he's never said so." I answered.

"Why would he be afraid?" asked Virginia.

"I don't know. Maybe he's just shy or I'm wrong." I made it to my feet but felt about twenty pounds heavier.

Between mug-ups and dinner won't be hungry for a long time. Wonder how long?

His daughter was starting the dishes, taking hot water from the stove to pour into the sink.

"Would you like some help with the dishes? The least I can do for all the food." I asked.

Ed answered "No, you have work to do. It was our pleasure to have you as a guest."

"Thank you again everyone. Bye for now." I gave Ed a parting handshake. *Hope this isn't the last time.*

Virginia walked out into the post office with me, crossing the room ahead of me and looking out the door. "It's safe. Cindy is gone. Hope you forget people like her. Bye, nice having you."

"Thank you." I stepped out into the sunshine. Another perfect day, I strolled along towards the Wahoo with its bow beached about one hundred yards away. At fifty yards an arm slithered around my waist.

"Hello, Honey please stay. I'm greatest in or out of bed. I can sing too." Cindy whispered in my ear.

I pulled her arm free rather roughly. "Cindy, that's great and I hope you find a lover who wants your songs and gold. I just don't. Do you understand?" We had reached the Wahoo's anchor, which was stabbed into the beach to hold the boat in case the river rose. I tossed the briefcase onto the bow deck. Bent to pick-up the anchor, Cindy grabbed me by the crotch in front and belt in the back.

"Right on, hard on." She hollered and we tumbled onto the muddy beach. She managed to unfasten my belt as she pulled my shirt out of my pants. We rolled on the soft mud beach, struggling.

I can't hit a woman. Even if she is no lady. Criminy never thought I'd fight to save my virtue. Remember wrestling moves. I managed to execute one of the escape moves I'd learned in high school wrestling. Which left

Cindy face down. Instead of the follow-up move straddling my opponent, I grabbed the anchor made it to the Wahoo. I could hear laughter. Looking up, I saw George through the plexiglass windscreen. Or rather I saw George's tonsils. Cindy was scrabbling up off the muddy beach. *Bastard is really enjoying this.* He could help. **How?** *What's this. Shit she's back.*

Cindy's arms were around my waist. "You can't go until I sing Green River for you!"

Green River, what the fuck is she talking about. Making like I'd intercepted a pass and had a defender hanging on me, I churned my feet against the mud, pushing the Wahoo off the beach. Cindy clinging to my waist, we followed the boat into the river. Laughing George had started the engines. He began backing up. I tried to lift myself onto the bow with my arms. Between Cindy and lunch, I found myself dangling from the bow. A woman pulling my pants down, her legs dragging in the water. Cindy dropped off standing in water up to her waist.

"Please listen to Green River before you go!" wailed Cindy.

I scrambled up onto the bow, my jeans down to my knees. As I turned on the bow to look back I could see Cindy's hands griping the bow as mine had. *Prepare to repel boarders!* I crawled to the edge looking down at Cindy's black hair.

"George, pull forward, we're too far out for her to drop off." George put the engine into forward and we moved gently ahead. I had taken Cindy's arms into my hands holding her up so she wouldn't drop into deep water. The expression on her face as she looked up at me went from one of alarm to satisfaction. George brought the boat into towards shore and I let go when he put the engine in reverse to stop our forward motion. Cindy's face changed to disappointment as she landed in ankle deep water.

"Please let me sing Green River for you?" she pleaded repeatedly, wadding deeper, following the boat, the water soon up to her breasts.

This is ridicules, give her a break. She'll drown if you don't. "George idle here while she sings? Then we'll go."

Surprisingly George, though his laughter did it. Gave a little touch of forward to stop our backward motion then we drifted downstream. Cindy with great enthusiasm began making a terrible noise. She was clearly pleased but I couldn't find a tune or pick out the words. I didn't know

Green River[55], country western I guessed. George's laughter increased, I was about to pop suppressing mine. Cindy was belting it out, wadding downstream matching our drift. *Current will sweep her away. Then will have to save her from drowning. She'll like that. My God I've never heard such terrible singing.* Laughter won over concern. I busted out, laughing so hard I thought I would lose lunch.

The wailing stopped. Cindy's face turned from a joyous performer to a dark evil face reminiscent of the devil's in Medieval paintings. The song was replaced by a chant, in a language I didn't recognize, with accompanying cabalistic hand motions that ended with both her arms dropping down and aiming at us.

At least she stopped the noise and wadding deeper. No water rescue. I went through the cabin and as I came out, still laughing, saying "George, I think she put a curse on us."

No longer laughing, he said "Your right. Let's leave." He hit the throttle and turned the boat downstream. "PING", the steering cable went slack as the wheel spun in George's hands. Moving aft to the outboards I grabbed the handle on the front of one of the engines which let me steer both.

I turned the boat back towards the village beach so we could make repairs. We both looked towards shore where a wet Cindy was still gesturing wildly.

"Let's pull in downstream away from the village." George answered "That's probably a good idea. Rain drops!" I said as we both looked up.

When did it cloud up? "You suppose her hex is working?" I said jokingly.

"Don't joke about it." George said, in concerned voice.

Cable breaks on an easy turn after many harder ones. First rain of the trip. Naw, no such thing as witches. Just coincidence.

We got soaked fixing the cable. Next morning it was still raining. Breakfast was cold as fast as it left the frying pan, which was popping and sizzling with rain drops.

"Well this sucks. Cindy said she was a devil woman. Maybe she is? What will happen next?" I said kidding.

George looking serious "She said she was a devil woman."

---

[55] Green River was a rock hit by Creedence Clearwater Revival, a favorite group of mine, I just didn't know it by name or recognize Cindy's rendition.

"Yeah, when she was trying to convince me to spend the winter with her. At least the coffee is hot. Bacon and eggs, floating in rainwater sucks." I answered. *Wonder if she really did have a cache of gold.*

We didn't have any more mechanical failures but it was cold and rainy for the rest of the trip.

OHAGAMUIT

In the rain we continued through Grayling, surveyed one of the most beautiful women I ever met, forgot to get her name. Anvik, Holly Cross and Russian Mission were uneventful, just cold and wet.

"George that's Ohagamuit coming up on the right. We should stop." I said.

"OK, how many surveys there?" He asked.

"None, it's a ghost town. Geiger said it was worth seeing. They had a fish wheel for tagging fish here once. The Yup'ik guy working for them wouldn't go into town because of the spirits." I explained.

"Sounds reasonable."

"Hey it stopped raining. Let's stop for a look. I've never seen a ghost town. You're not afraid of ghosts? They seem friendly, they stopped Cindy's rain." I said.

"No." But he sounded a little uncertain.

We landed and set the anchor. Luckily George did come with me, because I needed a conscious.

"What happened here? Looks like they just all left?" George asked.

"Geiger said the flu epidemic hit them really bad. Almost everyone died. The survivors decided the village was cursed, so they got out. Wonder how well received they were by the neighbors? Anyway, it's still considered cursed so no one touches anything. It just sit's and rots" I said.

"Will we catch the flu?" He wondered.

"Nah, it's surely long dead by now." [56] I answered. We peeked in the windows of a couple of the cabins. Pretty dark so couldn't see much.

"Damn, didn't think to bring a flashlight. I'll go back." I turned to return to the Wahoo.

"No. Don't think it's a good idea to swear here?" George reminded me.

---

[56] Many years latter researchers working at a flu abandoned village on the Seward Peninsula were able to recover viable flu virus.

He is superstitious. "Your right, the doors are mostly open. I'll just go in and have a look around. No, skunks in Alaska." I said.

"What about skunks?" George asked.

As I pushed into a cabin, the door was sticky, I answered "Abandoned houses and barns in the Midwest almost always have skunks living in them. Going in can be a stinky experience." I finished from inside. The cabin was empty, as were all the others I looked into. Several had collapsed or were on the verge of collapsing so I stayed out of them.

The Russian Orthodox church with it big onion shaped dome dominated town so we were drawn in that direction.

"Hope you don't get the flu?" George commented.

"Yeah, that would be awful. You'd have to do the surveys until I got well." *Wonder how long I could fake the flu? One village would be plenty.* On one side of the church was a wellkept cemetery. "Guess it's not completely abandoned. Someone is weeding the cemetery.

Inscriptions are always interesting. I'm going to have a look." I told George.

"You should stay out. Respect the dead."

"Sorry George, I'm just going to look at dates and inscriptions. Promise I won't walk on in anybody." To my surprise George followed me inside the low white picket fence. Many of the graves were individually fenced.

"Wonder if you have to be special to get a fence or just family tradition? Dates on the names seem to overlap so doesn't seem to be a change in style?" I wondered aloud. Most of the graves had Russian Orthodox crosses with small plates with the name and date of death. Some were just simple crosses made with two pieces of wood. A few had dates of birth, inscriptions or Bible verses. Most were weathered so badly they were barely legible. There were no stone markers, everything was wood. There were a few wooden head "stones", flat boards with varying degrees of decoration. One grave caught my eye, there was a flat rock at the base of the cross, on the rock was an antique glass bottle, the top resealed with wax. Inside was a perfect rose, the petals still red.

"George look at the bottle. What a souvenir!" I bent reaching for the bottle.

"No! Don't touch it. Would you want someone taking flowers from your grandmother's grave?" George asked.

That stopped me cold, my hand poised above the bottle. ***He's right.*** *What kind of thoughtless jerk are you turning into.* I stood up, without the bottle. "Just kidding, to see if I could get a rise out of you." I lied to cover up my moment of weakness. "Let's look at the church."

The door was actually locked but we could see the knave and pews through a couple of windows. It was very nice, icons on the wall, a magnificent gold cross behind the alter.

"That cross has to be painted, no way a real gold cross that size wouldn't have been taken by some greedy bastard." I said.

"Like you." George added.

Shit, doesn't need to rub it in. When he tells this story, he'll say I took the bottle. "Hey, I was kidding back there. You were right, it shouldn't be disturbed and I didn't. I didn't say I wanted the cross. I just don't think a solid gold one would still be here. What with the books of worship and good condition of the building they must still hold an occasional service and maintain the place."

"Yeah, we should probably be going." George said.

The rain started again as soon as we left Ohagamuit. *Cindy's curse didn't work there. Weird.*

MARSHALL

We traveled downriver to Marshall, another attractive wooded village. We tied-up at a small float plane dock. I marched out into the rain, briefcase safely under my raincoat and did a couple of undone surveys. Also stopped at the Hunter's just in case Bugsy, a friend from college, hadn't returned to the U of A yet. She had, I returned to the Wahoo and I saw several changes through my rain smeared glasses. First a tall kass'ak coming up the hill towards me, George standing in the rain watching the tall man and two nineteen-foot Grumman canoes tied to the Wahoo.

Always wanted one of those big canoes. Wonder what this guy wants.

"Hi. Your buddy tells me you just toured town. Can you tell me where the store is?" He said.

"Yeah." I said turning to face the village. "You just keep going uphill here towards the house with the Wein Air sign. The store is a couple of cabins further on. You can't miss it." "OK." He started walking. "Thanks." He said as an afterthought.

"Kim, do they have a post office?" George asked.

"Of course." *Could pretend I'm a Norwegian bachelor farmer and stop there.* "It's up the hill and next door to the Wein Air office. Did the gas guy come?" I asked.

"Yeah, I'll be right back." He slogged up the hill.

Good, worried I might have paid for undelivered gas. I hung up my raingear outside cabin door then stepped inside enjoying the heat provided by the small oil stove. We hadn't been using the stove. Until the curse in Kaltag. The recent cold nights and wet chilly days changed that. I jumped at a knock on the porthole, on the river side of the Wahoo! Turning I saw a beautiful water nymph, hair still wet from swimming, looking in the porthole.

"May I come in?" A muffled voice asked.

"Of course." *There goes the water nymph fantasy. Forgot the canoes.* I turned and opened the cabin door and a shivering soaking wet kass'ak woman came in through door. I helped her peel off a wet windbreaker. Thought she would burn herself as she practically hugged the stove.

Her wet shirt and skintight jeans left little doubt she was a babe. Bra less and ready to win a wet T-shirt completion. "Don't you have any rain gear?" I asked. *Glad she doesn't.*

"That's what his majesty is looking for at the store. It's going to come out of my share of course. Damn him! Answered an add in a magazine back home in California. Looking for a companion for canoe trip down Yukon River. Sounded like fun so I called. He says he's a writer and he'll sell the photos and story for big money to a magazine. I get ten percent if I finish the trip. He's going to sell the canoes in the last village to get money to go home. Fuck him. I'm tired of being cold and wet. Can you take me the rest of the way?" She blurted out through chattering teeth.

Ask a simple question. Wonder if sex was included for 10%? Should I ask? She really needs help. I could sleep on floor. She could have my bunk.

"Sure, he's not getting home by selling the canoes anyway. I worked in Emmonak at the mouth of the river all summer. All the villages down there are littered with canoes people had to leave who thought they would sell them at the end of the trip. Yup'iks are too smart for that. They know you can't afford to ship them out, they just wait till you leave. They get another canoe, they don't really need."

The boat rocked as George stepped aboard and into the crowded cabin. He saw the woman and stepped right back out signaling me to come. "Just a minute have to talk to my partner." I told my stove hugging guest.

I stepped out the door and grabbed my raincoat off the hook on the cabin wall. George and I huddled back by the outboards.

"Who's the girl?" Asked George.

"She's from the canoes. Guy got her to go on the trip down river under false pretenses. She wants to go on with us. What luck! I'll sleep on the floor. There'll be plenty of room." *Every time someone moves they'll step on you.*

"No!" George said.

"George it'll be great. She's gorgeous. She needs help." *He's right it's a stupid idea.*

"No. She doesn't work for Department. She can't be on the boat." George commanded.

He's right. _Damn it._ She still need's help. How? Got it. "OK. I'll go in and tell her she can't go with us." I went back into the cabin. "Sorry. You can't go. This boat belongs to the State of Alaska and we're on official business. I forgot. No passengers allowed. Would have been crowded anyway. I still have a solution for you. Get your stuff. I'll take you up to the Wein Air office and you can fly back to Bethel and on to California." I explained.

"I can fly out of here?" She asked in amazement.

"Yes, you could've flown out of any of the villages you stopped at." I said.

"That bastard! He told me the only air connection was at the end." A wet angry woman stormed out of the cabin and over the side into the canoes tied alongside. She ripped the tarps off finding her pack and jerking it out. She had everything rocking and rolling. Good thing we were tied to the dock. George had ducked into cabin.

"Let's go." She said with a fiery look in her eye. Then her face gentled, "Sorry, I'm mad at him not you, your trying to help. Please lead the way."

Maybe you should be mad at me. My lecherous side was trying to Shanghai you too a few minutes ago. "Here we go. Would you like to borrow George's raincoat?" I said without asking George.

"No, I can't get any wetter." She said climbing out of the boat.

We walked up the hill to the Wein Air office that was the first house at the top. "Hi. Have a passenger who needs to fly to Bethel and onto California." I told the agent, a plump middle aged Yup'ik woman. Following my lead, the dripping woman followed me in but headed straight for the oil heater against the back wall instead of the agent.

The agent behind the small desk ran out to her dripping passenger. "What happened you dear? Get to stove."

"I don't think she has any money, I can?" I started to say, uncertain if my checking account really could cover the ticket.

"Shush. Get out. I take care." _Obviously, she thinks I'm the cause._ The nymph's new protector ordered me out. I backed up to the far side of the room. While they whispered. They broke their huddle. The agent got a dry jacket off a hook for her, as nymph filled me in through her still chattering teeth.

"Thank you. She says I can get to Bethel on credit. I can call from their and arrange to pay for the tickets. Thanks, you've been a life saver." She slipped on the dry jacket and taking the stove in her arms instead of me.

O well, guess she'll get where she's going. Not even a kiss. "Bye." I said to her shivering back. I walked out and back down the hill. Where I could see the writer/photographer madly trying to fix the disarrayed tarps as he hollered at poor George.

"Here's Kim. He can tell you what happened?" George escaped into the cabin.

I walked across the Wahoo's work deck from dock to canoe side. "That's quite the rig. Two canoes lashed together. Improves stability but how do you paddle?" I asked innocently.

"Where's the bitch?" He snarled.

"The young woman was tired of being cold and wet. Plus, she wasn't too happy with you.

She's jumped ship. On her way home." I said in my imitation official voice.

He finished enclosing the interior of the canoes, balancing in the center open paddling station in the nearest one glaring at me "What gives you the right to interfere?"

If he wants to fight, no prob, he's got no footing, I'm higher, he does have that paddle.

Dazzle with bull shit. "I'm deputized by Alaska, not that I need to be to stop a kidnaping. Plus, I think the Feds might be interested. Isn't there a law about interstate transportation for immoral purposes?" I was guessing there had been some.

He fought to control his anger. Grounded the canoe paddle, to help his balance. "Hell.

Guess you did me a favor. I was tired of the whining bitch."

Pretty good bluff Kim old chap! "OK, we're leaving. You alright if we untie you or you need some help with your boats?" I asked.

"I'm leaving too. Just untie me forward there, if you would." He asked.

"Sure. Safe travels." I called as I tossed his bowline into the canoe. "Let's go George." George came out from behind the cabin door where he had been standing with the door cracked open. *Wonder in a fight if he would help. Probably. Like to think so.*

"You're the king of B.S., deputy sure." George said sarcastically.

"I am. Didn't they deputize you?" I asked.

"No, when did they do that?" George answered and asked.

"At orientation last spring, but I don't remember you being there. Shit, you missed all the fun." I said. *Even got to hold a shotgun on my friends.*

"You would have arrested that guy?" George wondered.

"No, they taught us to always get a real brown shirt[57] for that, but good bluff, took the fight right out of him." I said. The engines roared, as much as a twenty-five can. George adjusted the throttles as we passed the canoes to create the biggest wake possible.

"Wish we threw a bigger wake." He muttered as he adjusted the throttle to keep the Wahoo plowing water.

"Looks like you rocked him pretty good." *Guess he cared about the nymph too.* "He won't be able to sell those canoes like he plans. Wonder if their big enough for seal hunting this winter." I said.

"Seal hunting?" George asked surprised at the change in topic.

"Yeah, they like to tow a small skiff behind the snow machine. Not only makes good place for gear but when they get to an open lead in the ice they load the snow machine into the boat and cross. Those big freighters might be wide enough to take a snow machine." "Sounds cold to me." George commented.

"Yeah, I'm sure it is. I still would like to go some time." I said.

---

[57] Alaska's Fish and Wildlife Protection officers are specially trained State troopers. The FWP's wore a brown uniform, state troopers wore blue.

THE YUKON DELTA

Our next stops Pilot Station, Pitka's Point, St. Mary's and Mountain Village were uneventful. Just wet. The rain continued. It found every leak in the Wahoo's cabin and we were starting to wonder what it would feel like to be dry again. Seemed like everything was wet or damp. Sleeping bags, socks, and shorts, Huck Finn did it right, in the heat of a Midwest summer where the last thing you wanted was to be dry. Allo and Mike had completed the all of the Delta villages except Sheldon's Point where the Yukon and Bering Sea meet. They had tried to go one day but been driven back by strong winds and high waves.

George and I, although thoroughly tired of our trip down the Yukon, bypassed Emmonak and headed for Sheldon's to complete the survey. After Mountain Village the delta starts, it's just flat, covered with willows. There is nothing to stop the wind as it roars in off the Bering Sea. We made it past Sunshine Slough where I left a skiff sunk by waves back in June. The waves got worse. Had we been wise, like Mike and Allo, we would have turned back but we had a big solid boat and weren't going to let measly waves stop us. George was steering and I was the lookout since I had been to Flat Island and was certain I could pick Sheldon's Point out of the willows. We were regularly sinking the bow in the waves. Between looking for nearly invisible landmarks, I was regularly pumping the bilge. Finally, George said, hollering over the wind "We can't make it."

"OK, you won't get an argument from me." I hollered back.

George started the turn as we reached the "shelter" of the trough. The Wahoo crossed the trough and began quartering up the downwind wave. As the bow raised higher, the water in the bilge surged back spurting up through bilge pump-hole between the engines. I grabbed the bilge pump and once again began pumping like mad. My weight in the stern brought even more water gushing out onto the deck. *Have we sprung a leak!* SPLASH, gurgling the Wahoo's stern, weighted down with water, outboards and me, couldn't rise as fast as the following sea was overtaking us. Water was surging over the transom. I ran forward to George. The shift in weight helped but a sheet over water was still overtopping the transom. "More power." I screamed grabbing George by the shoulder and pointing to the sinking transom. He gave it all there was and slowly, at least it seemed slow, the stern raised on the wave. I ran back to the pump-hole and to my surprise there wasn't any water to be pumped. It all flowed forward in under the cabin now that the boat was running "downhill" on the wave. George was trying to steer the boat into the shelter of the north bank. As the bow rose again, the bilge water flowed back to the transom. I once again was able to pump water. The Wahoo actually seemed to hover, bow high quartering the wave to the north. Pumping finally yielded no more water. Almost simultaneously we finally crossed into the wind shadow on the north bank. Resuming a steady course towards the mouth of the Kwiguk Pass and Emmonak.

Cheated death again. *Thank you, Lord.*

Back in Emmonak we worked in the rain until after sundown. Unloading the Wahoo and slowly pulling it up into the boat yard with two Come-A-Longs. After a quick supper of SPAM, we spent the evening storing everything in the office attic. Once again crawling into damp sleeping bags for the night. In the morning, after eating the last pound of bacon for breakfast, we packed our damp personal gear in our packs. Dropped off the keys to the office at the AC store and walked to the airport. Where we caught the next plane to Bethel. We arrived in Bethel just in time for an Anchorage flight. In Anchorage George and I said goodbye.

Geiger picked me and the subsistence survey up at the airport. Too my surprise he took me to his house for a beer and to see his extensive collection of beer cans. Then dropped me at Phil's to pickup El Coyote, my land cruiser. He offered his hospitality for the night but I wanted to head towards Fairbanks. One last night in my damp sleeping bag somewhere between Anchorage and Fairbanks.

Kim Francisco

www.ingramcontent.com/pod-product-compliance
Lightning Source LLC
Chambersburg PA
CBHW051148120626
46547CB00012B/994